新国标应用型本科商务英语系列教材

总主编 王立非

跨文化交际实训

（双语）（第二版）

Intercultural Communication Practice

（Second Edition）

主编 刘重霄 刘 丽

编者 崔佳悦 郝 莉 陈媛媛

许冰莹 陈竞喆

对外经济贸易大学出版社

中国·北京

图书在版编目（CIP）数据

跨文化交际实训：双语 / 刘重霄，刘丽主编. —2版. —北京：对外经济贸易大学出版社，2023.3（2025.10 重印）

新国标应用型本科商务英语系列教材

ISBN 978-7-5663-2490-0

Ⅰ. ①跨… Ⅱ. ①刘…②刘… Ⅲ. ①文化交流–英语–高等学校–教材 Ⅳ. ①G115

中国国家版本馆 CIP 数据核字（2023）第 045471 号

跨文化交际实训（双语）（第二版）

Intercultural Communication Practice (Second Edition)

刘重霄　刘　丽　主编

责任编辑： 谭利彬

出版发行：对外经济贸易大学出版社	邮政编码：100029
社　　址：北京市朝阳区惠新东街 10 号	邮购电话：010－64492338
网　　址：www.uibep.com	发行部电话：010－64492342
资源网址：www.uibepresources.com	E-mail：uibep@126.com

成品尺寸：185mm×260mm	印　　刷：北京市泰锐印刷有限责任公司
印　　张：12.25	版　　次：2023 年 3 月北京第 2 版
字　　数：261 千字	印　　次：2025 年 10 月第 3 次印刷
ISBN 978-7-5663-2490-0	定　　价：49.00 元

“新国标应用型本科商务英语系列教材”
编　委　会

出版说明

党的二十大报告指出，中国积极参与全球治理体系改革和建设，践行共商共建共享的全球治理观，推动全球治理朝着更加公正合理的方向发展。中国呼吁世界各国弘扬全人类共同价值，促进各国人民相知相亲，尊重世界文明多样性，以文明交流超越文明隔阂、文明互鉴超越文明冲突、文明共存超越文明优越，共同应对各种全球性挑战。

习近平总书记强调，要大力培养掌握党和国家方针政策、具有全球视野、通晓国际规则、熟练运用外语、精通中外谈判和沟通的国际化人才。

教材是实现人才培养的基本工具和载体。“新国标应用型本科商务英语系列教材”是应对全球挑战、有效进行国际商务沟通、顺应国家现代教育改革的必然要求。2014 年 6 月 22 日国务院发布《关于加快发展现代职业教育的决定》（以下简称《决定》），全面部署加快发展现代职业教育。《决定》指出要“采取试点推动、示范引领等方式，引导一批普通本科高等学校向应用技术类型高等学校转型，重点举办本科职业教育。”

截至 2022 年 8 月，全国有 429 所高等院校开设了商务英语本科专业，其中多数院校属于应用型本科院校。本系列教材结合商务英语语言和教学的特点，融合多年商务英语教学实践，由长期从事商务英语教学一线的专家倾力打造，适用于全国应用型本科商务英语专业和财经类本科专业学生。

本套教材具有以下特色：

一、吸收二语习得和现代教育的最新理论，体现《商务英语专业本科教学质量国家标准》的最新要求。教材编写上注重提高学生的语言技能、让学生掌握相关的商务知识与实践技能，培养学生的跨文化交际能力、思辨与创新能力，以及自主学习能力。

二、秉承应用型本科教育“优化理论，突出实践”的理念。应用型本科教育注重技术但不能完全抛弃学术，其人才培养是学术性与职业性的有机统一，其基本特征是“本科底蕴+突出应用+专业特长”。体现在教材上，它强调“优化理论，突出实践”，优化理论基础，注重理论与专业技术的相关性，以培养目标与从业要求为依据对基础理论进行优化整合，介绍与专业相关的必要理论，重点强化行业知识的讲解；突出实践方面，强调教材的编排设计从教学目标到内容的组织，练习题的设计都环环相扣、注重培养学生的职业适应能力，突出实践教学的内涵。

三、贯彻“任务引领、项目导向”的指导思想。本套教材以“任务驱动”为理念，强化了教材的任务驱动效应，突出作业流程的可操作性；以真实企业业务经营为主线贯穿始终，从而保持教材内容前后的一致性和连续性；通过具体任务的设计和实施，使学生能够掌握业务技能。

对外经济贸易大学出版社
2023 年 1 月

前 言 | Preface

党的二十大提出，中国式现代化为人类实现现代化提供了新的选择，中国共产党和中国人民为解决人类面临的共同问题提供更多更好的中国智慧、中国方案、中国力量。

"人类命运共同体"理念，"一带一路"倡议的提出、践行与深化，促使全球范围内不同国家和地区的经济、政治、文化不断融合，人与人之间的交流与沟通更加频繁与深入。国际跨文化理论和实践也得到了进一步发展。这是中国展现负责任大国担当，积极参与全球治理体系改革和建设，积极建设覆盖全球的伙伴关系网络，推动构建新型国际关系的表现，也是在全球视域下构建当代中国哲学学科体系和中国国际学术话语权的重要举措，是中国式现代化的组成部分。

跨文化交际学，作为一门新兴的交叉学科，日益受到外语教育界的广泛关注。国内越来越多的高等院校，无论是专业外语还是公共外语，都开设了跨文化交际类课程。为了适应跨文化交际教学发展的需要，针对我国普通高校，特别是商务英语专业学生的具体情况和未来的职业需求，以外语专业和公共外语的《国标》及《教学指南》为指导与参照，我们编写了《跨文化交际实训（双语）》教材。本教材旨在通过跨文化交际知识介绍、经典案例分析和交际策略与技巧分享，提高学生的跨文化交际意识和能力。

本教材以党的二十大提出的办好人民满意的教育为宗旨，秉承教育是国之大计、党之大计的理念，融入外语教育培养什么人、怎样培养人、为谁培养人的思考，全面贯彻党的教育方针，落实立德树人根本任务。在教材编排和整体设计上方向正确，理论前沿，专业经典，逻辑清晰，内容丰富，特色鲜明，具体体现为：以具体的案例及分析培养学生的跨文化交际意识，以适宜的选材增加学生的跨文化知识，以多样性的课内外活动设计增加学生的跨文化情感体验，以实用的交际策略与技巧提高学生分析和解决问题的能力，最终实现跨文化交际综合能力的有效提升。本教材的部分案例来自编者或朋友的亲身经历，材料具有较强的真实感和现实性。

从结构安排上，本教材主要包括七个单元的内容，涵盖了跨文化的基本理论和必要的知识信息、跨文化交际的实际行为、跨文化商务实践以及有助于解决跨文化交际过程中所遇到的问题的策略与技巧。七个单元包含：Understanding Culture, Communication and Intercultural Communication；Cultural Patterns and Communication；Managing Intercultural Conflicts；Verbal Communication；Nonverbal Communication；Business Customs and Etiquette; Business Negotiation across Cultures。每单元都设有 Focused Study（主要进行基本理论、概念、知识信息介绍，包括文化背景知识、术语解释、词汇、思考题）、Case Study（具体的案例介绍与分析）、Extended Activity（与本单元内容相关的实践活动的延展）和 Further Reading（本单元知识点或相关理论的扩充）等环节。以上章节安排和内容设置都是基于当前跨文化交际理论研究的成果和编者多年教学实践的积累，希望能受到广大师生与学习者的欢迎。

同时，本教材配有练习题参考答案和教学课件资源。请登录 http://www.uibepresources.com 下载。

本教材由首都经济贸易大学外国语学院部分骨干教师参与编写。

由于水平有限，若有疏漏与不足之处，敬请广大专家与读者批评指正。

编　者

2022 年 12 月

目　录 Contents

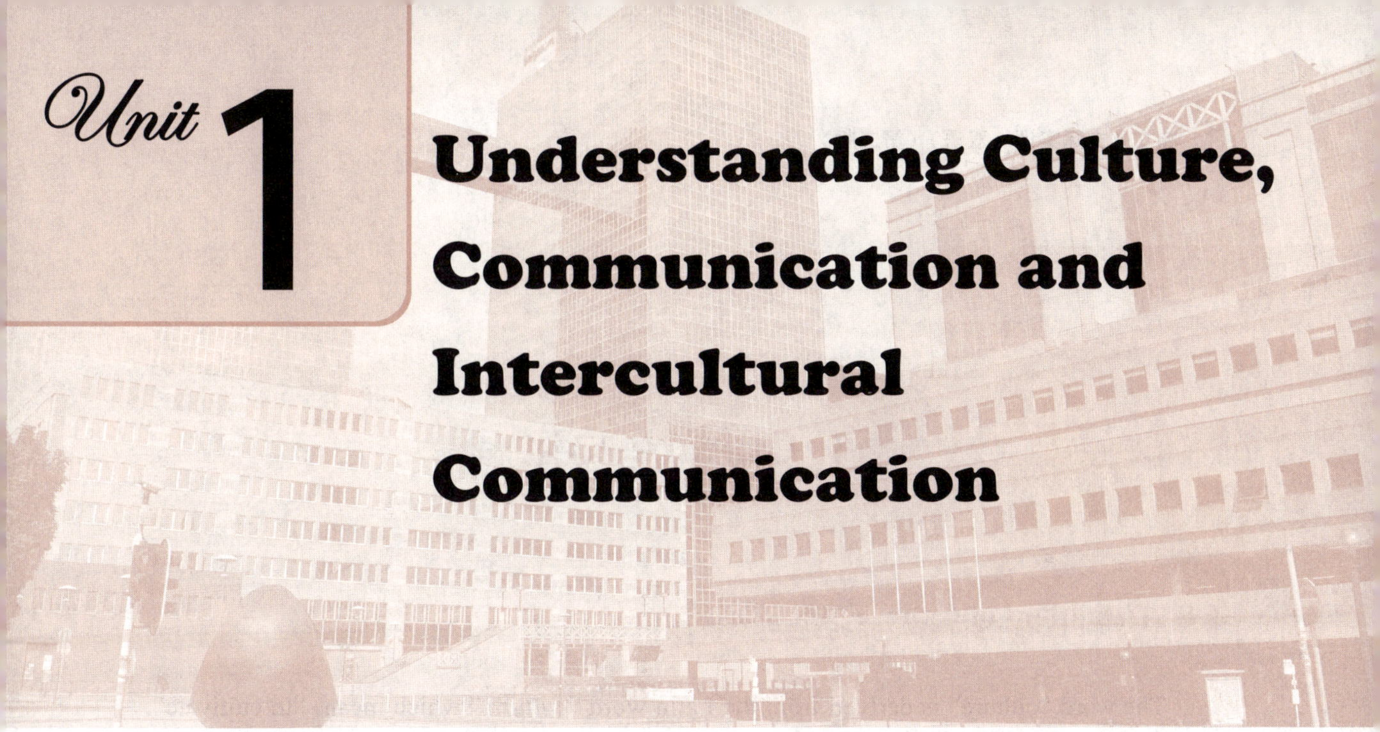

Unit 1 Understanding Culture, Communication and Intercultural Communication

Learning Objectives

After learning this unit, you will be able to:

- ✧ define characteristics of culture and communication;
- ✧ understand the relationship between culture and communication;
- ✧ define and classify the types of intercultural communication.

Warm-up

1. What is culture in your view?
2. How can people from different cultures communicate with each other?
3. What will get in the way when people from different cultures communicate with each other?

Focused Study

1. Culture 文化

1.1 Definitions of Culture 文化的定义

The word "culture" is derived from the Latin word "*cultura*" which means "to cultivate". Culture follows us anytime and anywhere. Culture lives in the past as well as in the present. Man is born and brought up in a specific cultural environment. Cultures are not uniform and every society has its own unique culture. Cultural elements like customs, traditions, morale, values, and beliefs, are not the same everywhere. Meanwhile, one culture also varies from time to time.

The scope of culture is very inclusive. According to general statistics, there exist hundreds of definitions about culture. Many scholars have defined and understood culture in various ways for many years. There are some famous ones among those definitions. The English anthropologist Edward Tylor was the first one to coin the term "culture" in the eighteenth century. He defined culture in 1871 as:

> *the outward expression of a unifying and consistent vision brought by a particular community to its confrontation with such core issues as the origins of the cosmos, the harsh unpredictability of the natural environment, the nature of society and humankind's place in the order of things (Cohen, 1991).*

Kroeber and Kluckhohn (1952) express their opinion:

> *Culture consists of patterns, explicit and implicit, of and for behavior acquired and transmitted by symbols, constituting the distinctive achievement of human groups, including their embodiment in artifacts; the essential core of culture consists of traditional (i.e. historically derived and selected) ideas and especially their attached values; culture systems may, on the one hand, be considered as products of action, on the other as conditioning elements of further action.*

Edward Hall was a pioneer researcher in intercultural communication field. He understood culture as follows:

Culture (is) those deep, common, unstated experiences which members of a given culture share, which they communicate without knowing, and which from the backdrop against which all other events are judged (Hall, 1966).

Bates and Plog propose a descriptive definition:

Culture is a system of shared beliefs, values, customs, behaviors, and artifacts that the members of a society use to cope with their world and with one another, and that are transmitted from generation to generation through learning.

This definition includes not only patterns of behavior but also patterns of thought (shared meanings that the members of a society attach to various phenomena, natural and intellectual, including religion and ideologies), artifacts (tools, pottery, houses, machines, works of art), and the culturally transmitted skills and techniques used to make the artifacts (Bates & Plog, 1990).

From the more recent perspective we highlight the definition of Hofstede who stated that, "culture refers to the cumulative deposit of knowledge, experience, beliefs, values, attitudes, meanings, hierarchies, religion, notions of time, roles, spatial relations, concepts of the universe, and material objects and possessions acquired by a group of people in the course of generations through individual and group striving" (Hofstede, 1997). In this book, we intend to use this definition because it is more comprehensive and inclusive.

Iris Varner and Linda Beamer (2006) think, "culture is the coherent, learned, shared view of a group of people about life's concerns that ranks what is important, furnishes attitudes about what things are appropriate, and dictates behavior".

Spencer-Oatey (2008) writes, "culture is a fuzzy set of basic assumptions and values, orientations to life, belief, policies, procedures and behavioural conventions that are shared by a group of people, and that influence (but do not determine) each member's behaviour and his/her interpretations of the 'meaning' of other people's behaviour".

1.2 Layers of Culture 文化分层

Culture can be manifested at different layers of depth. Trompenaars and Turner suggest a more insightful way of viewing culture. They describe a multi-layered model of culture in which three main areas are identified. The outmost layer of culture includes explicit products of a culture, which are easily observed and constitute "symbols of a deeper level of culture" (Trompenaars and Turner, 1994). The core encompasses basic assumptions about life and the world, and implicit ways of dealing with all aspects of human existence. The middle layer is made of norms and values, and determines what behaviours are interpreted as right or wrong, good or bad. Getting to know, understand and respect norms and values observed by a different cultural group is a fundamental step towards becoming effective intercultural communicators (Scherer & Walbott, 1994).

A similar view is expressed by Hofstede (1994), who identifies four main layers of culture that is known as "onion diagram" (see Figure 1-1). Hofstede describes the four layers of culture in Figure 1-1 as:

1. Culture symbols

Symbols are the most visible and superficial part of a culture that can be seen by others of the same and differing cultures. Symbols are those objects, words and gestures that mean something and are recognised by those sharing the same culture. Examples of symbols include jargon, hairstyles, Coca-Cola, religious and status symbols. With time old symbols may give way to newer more fashionable symbols. Being superficial they are easily copied by individuals belonging to other cultures.

2. Culture heroes

Culture heroes are those persons, dead, alive, real or imaginary that exhibit characteristics that are well respected within that culture. Heroes range from presidents to comic book characters.

3. Culture rituals

Rituals are those practices that are exercised by members of a culture that are considered socially essential. Examples of rituals include handshaking when meeting someone, religious ceremonies and the way in which business and other meetings are conducted.

4. Culture values

Unlike culture symbols, culture values are not visible to an observer. Hofstede (1994) describes values as a "feeling with an arrow attached to it" such as evil versus good, dirty versus clean, ugly versus beautiful, natural-unnatural. Many values remain unconscious to those who hold them. Therefore, they often cannot be discussed, nor can they be directly observed by others. Values can only be inferred from the way people act under different circumstances.

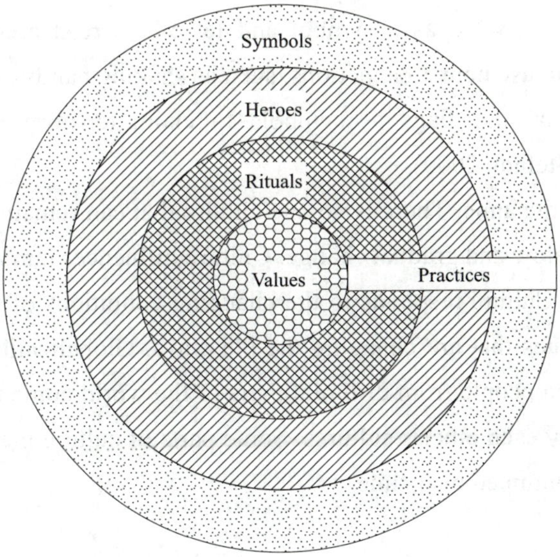

Figure 1-1 Manifestations of Culture at Different Levels of Depth

1.3 Characteristics of Culture 文化的特征

Regardless of various definitions of culture, a number of characteristics of culture have been drawn attention to. We here focus on four important points.

First, culture is learned. We learn culture through enculturation. Enculturation is conscious or unconscious conditioning occurring within that process whereby the individual, as child and adult, achieves competence in a particular culture (Hoebel & Frost, 1976). Therefore, we learn culture consciously or unconsciously. From infancy, members of a culture learn their patterns of behavior and ways of thinking until most of them become internalized and habitual. Interaction, observation and imitation are main ways for us to enculturate ourselves to one particular culture.

Second, culture is transmitted across generations. Culture is left from those who lived before us and handed to us. Cultural components like values, beliefs and traditions can be transferred across generations in the form of symbols. Besides, art, music and dance are all parts of culture that are also transmitted across generations. The past has shaped our present and is going to influence our future. The future generations learn to adopt the culture passed down from their forefathers.

Third, culture is based on symbols. The way we see the world is based on symbols and the meaning behind those symbols. The symbols any culture employs take a variety of forms. Cultures can use the spoken word as a symbol and tell people about the importance of freedom.

They can use the written word as a symbol and let others read about such as the War of Independence. They can use nonverbal actions, such as shaking hands or bowing, as symbols to greet another. They can use flags as symbols to claim territory or demonstrate loyalty (Samovar, Porter and Stefani, 2000).

Fourth, culture is dynamic. There is no one culture that can remain in the permanent state. Culture is subject to a slow and gradual change. Culture influences human, but human activities also influence culture. Culture responds to the changing conditions of the world, such as new ideas and new techniques that are changing the old ways. Globalization leads to a mixing of different cultures. When people from different parts of the world come together, they influence each other and certainly each other's cultures. Some parts of culture may evolve into new ones and some may be discontinued over time.

Key Terms

1. culture 文化

很多学者曾表达过自己对文化的理解，因此对文化的定义颇多。荷兰著名文化学者霍夫斯塔德对文化的定义较为全面，更具有包容性，因此本书采用了他的观点，即“文化指的是在世世代代社会中的一个群体，通过个人和群体的努力，对知识、经验、信仰、价值观念、态度、意义、等级、宗教、时间观念、角色、空间关系、宇宙观、实物与物质财富的累积存储。”这一文化定义既涵盖了精神领域，也涵盖了物质领域。

2. layers of culture 文化分层

根据文化中各个组成元素的显见程度，我们可以把文化分成几个深浅程度不同的层次，如同洋葱一般。因此，文化分层模型通常被称为“洋葱模型”。琼潘纳斯和特纳把文化分为外层、中间层和核心层三层。文化的外层是指不同文化的外在表现。文化的中层是指社会道德行为标准和价值观念。文化的核心是指不同文化有不同解决问题的方式。霍夫斯塔德的“文化洋葱模型”把文化分为象征物、英雄、礼仪和价值观四层。象征物指的是文化中最容易看到的表层部分，如语言和发型。英雄指文化中人们所尊崇的人物性格，上至总统，下至喜剧书中的人物性格。文化礼仪指某一文化群体的行为惯例，被认为是社会的根本。文化价值观不易被察觉，其实质是人们理解和秉持真善美的观念。

3. characteristics of culture 文化的特征

文化的主要特征包括以下四点：一、文化是可以学习的；二、文化是可以传承的；三、文化是以符号为基础的；四、文化是动态发展的。

Glossary

cultivate	*v.* 耕作；种植；教养；栽培
inclusive	*adj.* 包括的；包罗广泛的
anthropologist	*n.* 人类学家
consistent	*adj.* 一致的；连续的；不矛盾的；坚持的
cosmos	*n.* 宇宙
unpredictability	*n.* 不可预测性
explicit	*adj.* 明确的；清楚的；直言的
implicit	*adj.* 不言明的；含蓄的；无疑问的；绝对的；内含的
transmit	*v.* 传送；传递；传输；发射
distinctive	*adj.* 独特；有特色的；与众不同的；区别的
embodiment	*n.* 体现；化身；具体化
artifact	*n.* 人工制品；手工艺品；加工品
backdrop	*n.* 背景
cumulative	*adj.* 累积的；渐增的；追加的
spatial	*adj.* 空间的；存在于空间的；受空间条件限制的
fuzzy	*adj.* 模糊的；绒毛般的；含糊不清的
encompass	*v.* 围绕；包围
jargon	*n.* 行话；行业术语；黑话
enculturation	*n.* 对某种文化的适应；濡化
internalize	*v.* 使内化；使藏在心底
dynamic	*adj.* 动态的；动力的；充满活力的；不断变化的

Comprehension Questions

1. How do scholars elaborate on culture?
2. What are the elements of each layer of culture?
3. What are the major characteristics of culture?

2. Communication 交际

2.1 Definitions of Communication 交际的定义

Communication is closely connected with culture and they are inseparable. Edward Hall (1977) said, “Culture is communication and communication is culture.” Communication is viewed as an element of culture. Communication practices will definitely change as cultures are different. One particular culture leads to a particular mode of communication. Contact of human is based in communication. Without communication human cannot exchange their information and make progress in the world.

Just as it is not easy to define culture, so it is hard to give communication a unique definition. 126 definitions of communication were found by Dance and Larson (1972) in their research. J. T. Wood (1989) said, “Communication is a dynamic, systematic progress in which meanings are created and reflected in human interaction with symbols.” We prefer to use this definition in the book with regard to its closeness to the features of communication. G. G. Brown suggests, “Communication is transfer of information from one person to another, whether or not it elicits confidence. But the information transferred must be understandable to the receiver.” Fred G. Meyer presents a simple definition of communication, that is “Communication is the intercourse by words, letters or messages.”

2.2 Primary Types of Communication 交际的基本类型

When we communicate with one another, there are many ways by which we use to convey the message, among which verbal communication, nonverbal communication, written communication and visual communication are basic. Information, messages, opinions, thoughts, etc., can be exchanged with the aid of different communicative aids such as books, laptops and smart phones.

Verbal communication simply implies communication by sending a message through a spoken language. Speaking is an effective channel for people to communicate with each other spontaneously. The message should be understood by both the sender and receiver. For example, face-to-face interview, listening to a lecture, or listening to a television program.

Rather, without having to use words, nonverbal communication involves physical ways of communication to express feelings, emotions, attitudes, and thoughts. Gestures, facial expressions, body movements and so on, are applied in nonverbal communication like eye-contact, posture, touch and tone of voice. Some arts such as music and dancing are also aesthetic nonverbal forms of communication.

Written communication is sending a message with the help of written words in letters, e-mails, notices, reports, articles and memos. Written communication seems more formal and reliable than verbal communication like speech. Unlike other types of communication, written messages can be edited and rectified before it is sent to the receiver. Written communication will also cause some delay and take time to complete as feedback is not immediate like verbal or nonverbal communication.

Visual communication involves the visual display of information, wherein the message is understood or expressed with the help of visual aids. For example, topography, photography, signs, maps, colors and posters help the viewer understand the message visually. Movies and television shows and video clips are all electronic form of visual communication. Visual communication also involves the transfer of information in the form of text, which is received through an electronic medium such as a computer, phone, etc. Icons and emoticons are also a form of visual communication. When these icons are used in a public place, phone or computer, they instruct the user about their meaning and usage. The World Wide Web communicates with the masses, using a combination of text, design, links, images, and color.

2.3 Components and Process of Communication 交际元素和交际过程

A basic communication process consists of seven major components: (1) sender, (2) message, (3) encoding, (4) medium, (5) receiver, (6) decoding, and (7) feedback (see Figure 1-2). The communication process is not static but dynamic in nature and is both affecting and being affected by many variables, among which the context in which communication takes place is of vital importance. Every communication proceeds with context. The sender chooses the message to communicate within a context. Context may be physical, social, chronological or cultural.

1. Sender

Sender, known as encoder, is a person who intends to makes use of symbols to convey a message to others. Sender may be an individual, a group or an organization. The views, background, approaches, skills, competencies, and knowledge of the sender have a great impact on the message.

2. Message

Message is the content of communication that the sender wants to convey. Message must be understood by the receiver in same terms as intended by the sender. Each message has its purposes—maybe an opinion, attitude, feeling, greeting, decision or order, etc. It may take forms of verbal, nonverbal, written and visual signals.

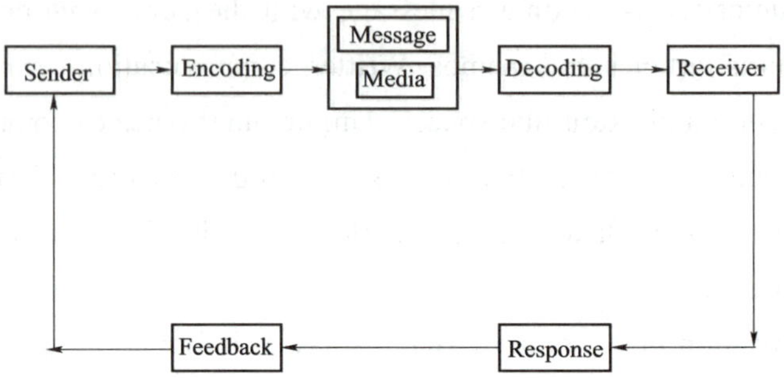

Figure 1-2 Main Components of Communication Process

3. Encoding

Since the subject matter of communication is theoretical and intangible, its further passing requires use of certain symbols. Conversion of the subject matter into these symbols and organizing them is the process of encoding. This can be encoded into words, nonverbal symbols, pictures, etc.

4. Medium

Medium is a channel which is used to transmit the message to the receiver. The sender must choose an appropriate medium for sending the required information. The choice of medium may depend upon the features of communication. For instance, written medium is chosen when a message has to be conveyed to a small group of people, while an oral medium may be chosen when spontaneous feedback is required from the recipient as misunderstandings are cleared then and there.

5. Receiver

Receiver, or decoder, is a person who receives the message or for whom the message is intended or targeted. The receiver must try to understand the message and achieve the desired objective. The degree to which the receiver understands the message depends upon various factors such as knowledge of recipient, their responsiveness to the message, and the reliance of senders on receivers.

6. Decoding

Decoding is opposed to encoding. It is the process that the receiver tries to convert the symbols received into meanings and extract the content of message.

7. Feedback

Communication is a two-way interaction. Hence, feedback is an essential component of communication. It is any response to a communicated message. On one hand, feedback may help the sender to make any necessary adjustments so that the message is correctly received; on the other hand, it may produce further clarification or discussion. Feedback may appear verbally, nonverbally or visually, etc. Feedback may be positive or negative. Positive feedback indicates the receiver has received and understood the message. Negative feedback indicates that the receiver either has not received the message or has not understood its content.

Key Terms

1. communication 交际

正如文化定义的多样性一样，交际的定义也繁多。鉴于伍德的交际定义更接近交际本身的特征，本书倾向于使用这一定义，即“交际是人类创建语义并通过符号反映到人类活动中的一个动态的、系统的过程。”

2. primary types of communication 交际的基本类型

当人们相互交际时，通常会采用四种基本的交际类型——言语交际、非言语交际、书面交际和视觉交际。

3. components of communication 交际元素

基本的交际包括七个主要的组成元素——发送者、信息、编码、媒介、接受者、解码和反馈，并且这七个组成元素相互关联、相互作用，完成整个交际。交际过程本质上是动态的，而非静止的。

Glossary

elicit	*v.* 引出；探出；诱出
intercourse	*n.* 交流；交往；交际
spontaneously	*adv.* 自然地；自发地；不由自主地
aesthetic	*adj.* 审美的；美的；美学的；具有审美情趣的
transcript	*n.* 抄本；副本；誊本
topography	*n.* 地貌；地形学
photography	*n.* 摄影；摄影术
icon	*n.* 偶像；崇拜对象；图标；圣像
emoticon	*n.* 情感符

variable	*n.* 可变因素；变量
	adj. 变化的；可变的；变量的；变异的
chronological	*adj.* 按时间的前后顺序排列的；编年的
responsiveness	*n.* 响应性；易起反应

Comprehension Questions

1. How is culture interrelated with communication?
2. How do scholars define communication? And how do you define it?
3. What are the basic types of communication?
4. Can you describe how communication occurs?

3. Intercultural Communication
跨文化交际

3.1 Definitions of Intercultural Communication 跨文化交际的定义

Among numerous definitions of intercultural communication, one proposed by Samovar, Porter and Stefani (2000) is typical, "Intercultural communication is communication between people whose cultural perceptions and symbol systems are distinct enough to alter the communication event." This definition is often quoted by people. According to Ting-Toomey (2007), intercultural communication is "the symbolic exchange process whereby individuals from two or more different cultural communities negotiate shared meanings in an interactive situation".

The term "cross-culture" is always misunderstood as "intercultural communication". It is necessary to distinguish these two terms. The term "cross-culture" is used in the intercultural literature to refer to the communication process that is comparative in nature (e.g., comparing conflict styles in culture X, Y and Z), while the term "intercultural" is used to refer to the communication process between members of different cultural communities (e.g., business negotiation between a Dutch importer and an Indonesian exporter) (Ting-Toomey, 2007). It is clear that intercultural communication is conducted between members from different cultural groups. The potential for misunderstanding, disagreement and even conflicts is almost guaranteed because of cultural differences in different contexts. In order to reduce the risk, it is very necessary to study intercultural communication.

3.2 The Forms of Intercultural Communication 跨文化交际的类型

The labels *race, ethnic group and intracultural communication* are often used in discussions of intercultural communication. All three of these are actually forms of intercultural communication.

1. Interracial communication

Interracial communication occurs when the source and the receiver exchanging messages are from different races. Most of scholars reserve the word race for physical features rather than cultural traits. Some arguments support that race will not be distinct enough to warrant separate categories because physical traits are beginning to blend. However, we cannot deny that physical differences frequently do influence communication. It is often reflected through strong prejudice and leads to stereotyping and discrimination.

2. Interethnic communication

Ethnic groups usually form their own communities in a country or culture. They share a common origin or heritage that is apt to influence their family names, language, religion, values, and the like. For instance, the Chinese in San Francisco and the Mexicans in San Diego might be citizens of the United States, but their ethnic cultures are transferred intergenerationally. This enables them to preserve their identities to some degree, though they still live within the American dominant culture (the culture in power or the mainstream culture).

3. Intracultural communication

Intracultural communication is often used to define the exchange of messages between members of the dominant culture. It also refers to the communication in which one or both participants hold dual or multiple memberships. In these cases, racial, ethnic, or other such factors also come to play (Samovar, Porter & Stefani, 2008).

It is believed that interracial, interethnic, and intracultural communications all share the same process and elements. In other words, specialized alliances and associations create shared perceptions, comparable norms and values, and distinctive verbal and nonverbal codes. Therefore, the term intercultural communication seems to be the best choice to represent the interaction process.

3.3 Main Barriers in Intercultural Communication 跨文化交际的主要障碍

With the rapid spread of globalization in the 21st century, it becomes urgent for us to understand people with diverse cultural backgrounds. Intercultural communication comes on the stage under this situation. During communication people are inclined to interpret messages from their own perspectives. They unconsciously or consciously behave the way their culture guides them. This could bring about greater misunderstanding or conflicts. Knowing the barriers of intercultural communication is the first step to overcome potential problems. Among these problems, language ranks the first.

1. Language

Language is a fundamental tool that we use to interact with one another. "Language gives people a means of interacting with other members of their culture and a means of thinking. Language thus serves both as a mechanism for communication and as a guide to social reality." (Samovar & Porter, 1982)

Different languages can produce an obvious barrier to intercultural communication. It may entirely lead to communication breakdown. For instance, if you were in America and could only speak Chinese, you would catch a feeling that you are blind and dumb as you won't be able to communicate with Americans verbally. Even if you had studied English, different English accents and slangs could still cause communication problems. Additionally, words don't necessarily translate from one language to another in a clean one-to-one correspondence. Poor writing is proving to be a greater barrier than poor talking.

In addition, nonverbal language is also an underlying barrier to intercultural communication that is always neglected. People of one culture might find a particular gesture as offensive as compared to other countries' cultures. Level of eye contact, distance between two people while making a formal vs. informal communication are such examples of situations one must study about before starting an intercultural communication. In China while exchanging visiting card, one must accept it with both hands and have a good look at the card. One should not keep it in his/her pocket immediately.

2. Negative stereotypes

Stereotypes are grossly oversimplified and overgeneralized abstractions about groups of people and are usually highly inaccurate although they may contain a grain of truth (Pennington, 1986). Examples abound, of course. For example, English people are conservative, polite and formal, while French people are romantic, artistic and arrogant. Many researchers argue that stereotypes are by nature harmful because they lead to the ignoring of the individuality of individual members of other cultures and create expectations and self-fulfilling prophecies to the detriment of the individual concerned (Gudykunst, 2004). We call them negative stereotypes. In intercultural communication people easily treat group members of a different culture as having certain invariable and fixed properties, and as being essentially different from members of other groups. Yet they only have few or no essential features; they only have identifying and ascribed features that just have a probabilistic association, of varying degrees of strength, with a particular group (Spencer-Oatey & Franklin, 2010).

3. Prejudice and discrimination

Compared with harmful stereotypes, prejudice and discrimination about people from other cultures can cause more serious intercultural communication problems and give real offense. Prejudice can be defined as the set of affective reactions we have toward people as a function of their category memberships (Schneider, 2004). Discrimination is worse than stereotypes and prejudice. It refers to the treatment of a person or a group of people unfairly or differently because of their membership of a particular social group (Chryssochoou, 2004). The following examples display the differences of stereotypes, prejudice and discrimination in comparison. Negative stereotypes: members of Group X are lazy, unreliable and slovenly. Prejudiced attitude: I don't like (people who belong to) Group X. Discrimination: I prefer to exclude them from the neighbourhood, avoid hiring them, etc. (Jones, 2002). It is thought that stereotypes lead to prejudice, and prejudice leads to discrimination, and then discrimination leads to exclusion and inequality. They are interrelated and unidirectional, but all of them are deadly threats toward intercultural communication.

4. Ethnocentrism

Ethnocentrism, or a belief that one's own culture is better than that of others, can lead to acting superior toward other groups and not treating them well.

5. Values

Values mean different in different sentences. Communication breakdown occurs if there is wrong perception by the receiver.

Key Terms

1. intercultural communication 跨文化交际

跨文化交际指的是人们之间的文化观念和符号体系差异足以改变交际事件的交流。

2. interracial communication 跨种族交际

跨种族交际指的是不同种族的发送者和接收者之间的信息交流。

3. interethnic communication 跨族群交际

跨族群交际指的是来自同一国家或文化的各族群之间的交流。每个族群通常拥有共同的起源或遗产，对他们的姓氏、语言、宗教、价值观等诸如此类的方面有着一定的影响。

4. intracultural communication 同文化交际

同文化交际，或称作内文化交际，指的是主流文化成员之间的信息交流，也指交际一方或双方拥有双重或多重身份之间的交流。

Glossary

warrant	*v.* 保证；担保；授权；批准；辩解
	n. 授权证；许可证；正当理由；依据
intergenerationally	*adv.* 代际地
dominant	*adj.* 占优势的；统治的；支配的
mechanism	*n.* 机制；机能；（机械）结构
stereotype	*n.* 固定形象；刻板印象；陈规旧习；铅版
abound	*v.* 丰富；充满；大量存在
prophecy	*n.* 预言；预言书
detriment	*n.* 损害；伤害
slovenly	*adj.* 邋遢的；懒散的；疏忽的
exclusion	*n.* 排除；排外主义；拒绝
unidirectional	*adj.* 单向的；单向性的

Comprehension Questions

1. Is intercultural communication identical to cross-cultural communication? Please explain the reasons.
2. What are the main barriers in intercultural communication?
3. How are stereotype, prejudice and discrimination connected with each other?

Extended Activities

Case Analysis

Case 1

Dog Meat Eating Festival: Tradition or Torture?

One of the strangest traditions in Chinese culinary heritage is the oft-battled Dog Meat Eating Festival, which occurs in many regions throughout southern China.

This Festival occurs on the Summer Solstice and is a tradition with over 600 years of history behind it. The exotic, alleged delicacy is served as a dog-meat hotpot with lychees and strong grain liquor. The preparation and consumption of this dish is performed with great reverence, as it is considered an elixir to ward off disease in the coming year. Over 10,000 dogs are eaten during this annual event.

This traditional event has been receiving increased resistance from animal rights groups over the years, and the festival has been banned in certain locations.

Animal rights activists claim that the dogs are treated cruelly and that is perverse to eat an animal that many keep as pets. Groups have posted graphic pictures of the dog butchering online and started mass petitions. Locals who want to keep the tradition alive state there is no strong difference between animals kept as livestock and animals kept as pets.

The Chinese people have a long history of consuming dog meat and it is considered to be a fortifying food for the ill. One local resident said, "We eat chicken, pork and beef, why not dog meat? I hope outsiders show some respect for our traditional festival." Another resident said, "It's unfair to call Yulin people brutal only because we have this tradition to eat dog meat. People who call us uncivilized and cruel should stop eating meat first."

Government officials kept tighter regulations on the festival this year to ensure that greater attention was paid to the humane treatment of the dogs and the festival continued amidst the protests.

(Source:http://gbtimes.com/life/dog-meat-eating-festival-tradition-or-torture)

Questions for Discussion

1. Some Yulin people argue that it is their old tradition to eat dog meat. Are they wrong to keep their tradition?
2. There is a serious conflict between people who love dogs and Yulin people who love eating dog meat. What suggestions would you offer to mediate or resolve this conflict?

Case 2

Saudi Arabia Orders Walls in Shops to Divide Male and Female Coworkers

The Saudi government has ordered that shops that employ both men and women to set up separation walls to ensure that the two sexes are separated while they work.

Stores must erect barriers not shorter than 1.6 meters to separate male and female employees. Retailers have 30 days to install the walls, or risk sanctions.

Essentially, women in Saudi Arabia can work either in all-women factories or in lingerie and cosmetics shops. The latter has been allowed since June 2011, when the Saudi leadership issued an order for lingerie and cosmetics shops to replace their male staffers, most of whom were Asian, with Saudi women.

As a result of the legislation, authorities announced that 44,000 jobs were created for Saudi women, for whom the unemployment rate currently stands at 36 percent, according to the country's Central Department of Statistics and Information. Saudi women account for only 7 percent of citizens employed by private companies.

The move followed complaints by Saudi women who felt uncomfortable buying lingerie or cosmetics from men. However, the decision to replace men with women also came under heavy criticism because of poor working environments for saleswomen, and cases of harassment.

Cultural attitudes towards women in Saudi Arabia are widely controversial, with the country known for its strict observation of Sharia law. At the beginning of 2013, women were allowed to participate in Shura Consultative council, with 30 appointed as counselors. However, they must use a separate entrance door.

Saudi women are generally forbidden from behavior that is common in Western cultures. The Gulf kingdom is the only country in the world that bars women from driving and voting, and they must have permission from a man to work, travel or open a bank account.

(Source: https://www.rt.com/news/saudi-women-walls-sexes-968/)

Questions for Discussion

1. What is the employment situation of women in Saudi Arabian? And what causes this consequence?
2. If you were a female foreigner in Saudi Arabia, would you behave the way that would do in your country? And why?

Activities

1. In small groups, each member tells about one or two of your communication problems with people from other countries. Make a list of these problems and try to provide some effective suggestions.

2. Investigate two or more foreigners and ask them how their cultures differ from Chinese culture. You may categorize their answers into several aspects, such as nonverbal behavior, religion, and values. Finally, make a comparison between Chinese culture and their cultures.

Further Reading

How Sensitive Is Intercultural Communication at the Workplace

The importance of intercultural communication in the workplace cannot, and should not be undermined. It plays an important role in the functioning of an organization and affects the final output too.

Though cross-cultural interaction is not new and has existed for ages, with the advent of globalization, the world has come close together. It is not surprising then that people have to travel to different parts of the world as a part of their job and have to adapt to that new environment. However, adaptation is not always easy, and a little support from colleagues goes a long way in easing the process of "fitting in" for the immigrant employees. This article explains to you the importance of intercultural communication in the workplace.

Important Factors

Intercultural communication mainly relates to issues pertaining to speech and culture of those belonging to an environment or land different from their own. It is obvious that a person who grows up in China is going to have a different culture than someone born and brought up in the United States. Even people from the United Kingdom find it difficult to adapt to the United States and vice versa, though these are seemingly similar countries and even speak the same language.

In the work environment, these cultures affect the behavior and values of the employees. How they respond to superiors, to colleagues and to subordinates, is all determined by the culture they have been bred in. Their attitude towards and their comprehension about their surroundings are also different. Their patterns of communication are varied and their concepts of formality and informality are different. For instance, several organizations address their bosses on a first name basis in the West. However, in other countries such as India, it is considered informal, so every superior is addressed as either "Sir" or "Ma'am".

It is when a person has to work in a country other than his own and is exposed to these changes, that he experiences a "culture shock". Culture shock is defined as the anxiety and disorientation experienced when a person is made to operate in an unknown culture. In such cases, programs that advocate intercultural communication and encourage healthy communication among employees belonging to various cultures, are required to help each other adjust easily. This is extremely important because the environment impacts the efficiency of employees, local or immigrant. The only way you can get the best out of them is to give them a positive environment that they can embrace and move on.

How to Aid Intercultural Communication in the Workplace

Miscommunication due to cultural barriers can be avoided and the process of adjustment for an immigrant employee can be eased if the organization makes an effort to make him feel welcome. Remember, he may already be having a tough time dealing with learning the language, or just adapting to such drastic changes. Anything that the organization can do to at least have his problems in the workplace sorted is helpful.

1. Maintaining a Positive Attitude

Before conducting an interaction with employees belonging to another culture, a little introspection is required. The employees of the dominant culture in the workplace need to identify their own attitude towards other cultures, and how this attitude is going to affect overall communication with those belonging to other cultures. This thought process is normally affected by certain prejudices and stereotypes, which have to be kept aside while interacting with immigrant employees and their abilities should be assessed at an individual level. Furthermore, taking for granted that all norms belonging to the dominant culture are understood is wrong. There has to be an effort in understanding the nuances of the immigrant employees' culture(s). All this can be done only by maintaining a positive attitude.

2. Understanding Diversity

It is important that employees of the dominant culture are educated about other cultures so that they are able to accept and understand the concept of diversity in the workplace. Just assuming that owning to citizenship of a particular country one becomes British or American is not acceptable. Any person carries his values, ethics and culture wherever he goes. If he is making an effort to understand the difference and accept cultural diversity in the workplace, so should the organization.

3. Encouraging Individual Interaction

Apart from educating employees, personal interaction with the immigrant employee to understand the nuances of his culture and explain the nuances of yours also makes a difference. A generalized study is never adequate or as effective as a one-to-one interaction. Furthermore, a person who is new to a culture, may fear interaction with other employees. It is the job of the organization to draw them out of their shell and genuinely include and accept them as part of the organization.

4. Conducting Induction Programs

The first phase after recruitment includes an induction program for employees. If these are held keeping immigrant employees in mind, it is going to ease the process for both, the organization and the employee. In this induction program, the organizational culture can be explained and the policies of the organization can be made clear. Even the office jargon is a part of daily functioning in the organization and should thus be explained to the immigrant employee. For instance, local employees know that the weekend comprises a Saturday and Sunday. However, for those belonging to the Middle East, the weekend comprises Friday and Saturday, and in fact, Sunday is the first working day. Such minor details should be made clear to the employee.

5. Discouraging Racism and Discrimination

Lastly, the best way to promote healthy intercultural communication is to discourage racism and discrimination by strongly advocating a non-racist policy. This will prevent any embarrassing situations that can lead to serious problems, among colleagues. While personal attitudes cannot be altered, workplace communication can be positive only if such rules are implemented.

Implementing the above-mentioned steps is sure to bring about the much required healthy intercultural communication in the workplace. Remember that all these will not only enhance the reputation of the organization and the country in the eyes of the immigrant employee, but he will embrace it willingly and give the job his best input.

(Source: http://www.buzzle.com/articles/intercultural-communication-in-the-workplace.html)

Unit 2 Cultural Patterns and Communication

Learning Objectives

After learning this unit, you will be able to:

✧ define culture values;

✧ describe the characteristics of culture values;

✧ make comparison between Chinese values and Western values.

Warm-up

1. Use some examples to explain the differences between Chinese and English religious beliefs.
2. List Hofstede's five values dimensions.

Focused Study

1. Culture Values 文化价值观

Values affect our behaviors in society fundamentally. They do not reflect on how we act in a culture but show what we ought not to do. Values provide standards for us and tend to be the basis of all the decisions we make to evaluate our own and others' actions. Thus a value can be defined as a conception, of the desirable which influences the selection form, available modes, means, and the ends of an action (王维波、车丽娟，2013).

Values are learned organizations of rules for making choices and for resolving conflicts. These rules and guideposts are normative and teach us what is good, right, useful, and wrong, how to live our life，what to strive for, and even what to die for. A value system represents what is expected or hoped for. It is not a report of actual conduct but it is the system of criteria for which sanctions are applied and conduct judged.

Values are useful in explaining and understanding cultural differences and similarities in behaviors; thus, understanding values and cultural basis is helpful in international business. If they understand how values vary from culture to culture, they are more likely to interpret and accept correctly behavioral differences. This acceptance and correct interpretation, in turn, enables you to interact effectively with others whose values and behaviors are different (王维波、车丽娟，2013).

Every culture has its own way of doing things in daily life, such as eating, dressing, drinking, making friends, finding shelters, marrying and dealing with death. People have to learn the cultural ways of their community to satisfy their basic human needs. These ways are not something that the people in the group are born with. Instinctive behavior, on the other hand, is a pattern of behavior that an animal is born with. For example, spiders spin their webs. The mother spider does not teach her babies how to spin. In fact, she is not even there when they are born. Young spiders know how to do it when they are born.

Most of the time, different customs of different cultures are neither right nor wrong. It is simply because that different people do things in different manners. Although each of us has a unique set of values, there are also values that tend to permeate a culture. These are called culture values (王维波、车丽娟，2013).

1.1 Comparison between Chinese Values and Western Values 中西价值观比较

Many scholars have written about cultural differences between the West and the East. Among these differences, three of them are highlighted here: cognition, the concept of truth and relationship with nature (William J. Seiler, 1992). Western people are said to incline to think in a linear fashion. A cause leads to an effect. In Eastern culture, a cause can be an effect and lead to an effect as well. Past, present and future are interconnected and affect one another. Eastern culture seeks harmony with nature while Western culture tends to be oriented toward mastery over nature. Regarding the concept of truth, the view of Western culture on ultimate truth or reality is based more on scientific and empirical explanation while that of Eastern culture is based more on existing truth. Cultural differences between the East and the West have a significant impact on the communication behavior and pattern. As a result of the differences in cognition, the concept of truth and relationship with nature, people from the West and the East are further different in the following aspects.

Differences in expressing gratitude. The Chinese and Westerners are different in expressing their gratitude. The Chinese who are close to each other seldom express their gratitude in public. Look at the following situation. A mother is busy in the kitchen, who suddenly asks her son to fetch a bowl for her. Then the son does so. The mother just continues cooking without any word of gratitude. Later at table, the mother hands her son a bowl of rice. The son just takes it and begins eating without any word of gratitude either. If such a situation happens in the United States, both the mother and her son will say "thanks" or "thank you" for fetching the bowl and serving the rice (王维波、车丽娟，2013).

Differences in symbolization. Symbolization is how people imagine or regard something. It actually reflects the way people think. The Chinese and Westerners are different in symbolizing. In the APEC summit held in Shanghai in 2001, Presidents from all over the world were invited to wear the traditional Chinese Tang suits for a photo together with the closing day coming. The Tang suits were ready and then the Presidents were asked to choose the colors of the suits by themselves. However, it was quite interesting to find that most of the Westerners preferred blue while most of the Easterners chose red. Red means luck and fortune in most Eastern cultures but stands for blood and revolutions in the West. Blue means something noble or significant in Western cultures (王维波、车丽娟，2013).

Differences in attitudes towards women. The Chinese and Westerners are different in attitudes toward women. "Ladies First" has a long history in the West. But in China there is no such a tradition. For example, a respectable elderly gentleman is having dinner with a young lady in a restaurant. In the West, it is likely the young lady who is first served because of their "Ladies First" tradition. But in China, it is normally the elderly man who gets the service first, because hierarchy is prevalent in China and it is the elderly or the superior who is supposed to get special respect.

With changes in women's roles, there have been changes in customs. Women used to expect that men would open doors for them, but now they open their own. When a man invited a woman out for dinner in the past, he was expected to pay for everything. Today, a woman might share the bill when she goes out with a man. She can be the one who calls a man up and asks him out. She may even pay for the entire date (高一虹，2000).

1.2 Comparison between Chinese Values and American Values 中美价值观比较

It is true that Chinese people and American people enjoy different cultures, which influence their lives, customs, aesthetics, behaviors and beliefs. The following is going to provide us with a better understanding of the differences between Chinese and American cultures.

Differences in friendship. Friendship means a lot to the Chinese. There is a Chinese saying: "One more friend, one more road." Whenever they have made friends with someone, they will try all their best to make the friendship as close as possible, and keep him/her as a lifelong friend. Lifelong friends feel deeply obligated to give the other whatever help might be required. However, Americans change their friends and acquaintances over time and have limited mutual obligation. They will try to help their friends in difficulty with some advice but avoid making a decision for them.

Differences in time consciousness. The Chinese relatively pay more attention to the past. They cherish old friends and classmates. If they happen to visit a city, they will squeeze their time to have a get-together with friends there. Americans usually are less interested in the past. Instead, they focus on what is going on for the time being. They believe that life is like a fast moving train.

Differences in conception of the self. Many Chinese are used to beginning their English conversation with "My English is poor." Because Chinese are collectivist, placing high value on group cooperation and individual modesty. Americans are individualists, placing high value on self-reliance and freedom from externally imposed constraints. At the beginning of a presentation, an American will say: "I believe that my presentation will be of great value to anybody present." (李君文，2000)

A Chinese visited an American friend in the United States. It was 11:00 p.m. He thought it was time for him to leave. Then he said, "Mr. Steve, it is too late. You should have a rest. I am sorry for having bothered you so much." The American friend angrily answered, "No, come on. I don't think you are bothering me. We had a good talk. Listen, if you want to go, it is because you want to go, not because of me."

Differences in approaches to tasks. The Chinese are relationship-oriented. They often maintain a harmonious relationship with some people, which has priority over accomplishing tasks. They don't care as much about timelines or schedules. Meetings may run long.

Americans are task-oriented. They focus on a scheduled timeline and would like to do one thing at a time. In their opinion, getting the work done is more important than relationships.

Differences in social relationships. The Chinese have hierarchical and formal social relationships. They feel uncomfortable while they are chatting with someone who holds a higher position. Americans have informal and egalitarian social relationships. People tend to minimize the importance of social rankings (杜学增，2000) .

1.3 Culture Values in International Business 国际商务中的文化价值观

In today's hyper-competitive global markets, any company that operates internationally is faced with the task of integrating many value systems into a framework that allows the organization not only to survive but also to compete effectively. The European Managerial Decision Making Project, which is a European research group, was formed in 1994 to examine the effect of different national value systems on organizational policy. The project's research methodology is simple: given identical business problems, do managers in six different European countries choose similar solutions? In addition to the responses to these questions, the study also includes both organizational and personal data (王维波、车丽娟，2013).

The behaviors that intrigue the research team most are decisions concerning payment selection, promotion, and what makes employees redundant are thought to reveal most about national values.

The researchers believe a strong bond exists between people's sense of well-being and their situation at work, that is, the way they get on with a work group or employer. For multinationals, therefore, an understanding of cultural diversity within the organization is prerequisite of effective employee relationships.

The research is based on semi-structured interviews with managers from 74 European banks. The managers are presented with common dilemmas focusing on four key areas: remuneration, recruitment, promotion and reductions in the workforce. The respondents are asked to solve these dilemmas and their reasoning.

The responses are then plotted between two opposing groups. The first logic is an economic rationale, which the researchers called "market logic". Here decisions are based on the economic realities arising from the marketplace as opposed to group considerations. The second logic is called "group logic". Even decisions such as who to promote or make redundant things can sometimes be discussed in terms of their group effects. According to the research, few people really know their culture values. This means that organizations need to take intercultural training seriously as it can be critical to the success of an international venture. Simply bringing in a "cultural expert" to talk about different national values is not an option (王维波、车丽娟，2013).

Glossary

explicit	*adj.* 明确的；清晰的
implicit	*adj.* 含蓄的；绝对的
intrigue	*v.* 欺骗；激起兴趣
symbolization	*n.* 象征；标志
hyper-competitive	*adj.* 极具竞争力的
recruitment	*n.* 招聘
rank	*n.* 等级；阶层；排列
oriented	*adj.* 以某为方向；以某为目的
remuneration	*n.* 报酬；酬劳；赔偿
methodology	*n.* 方法学

Comprehension Questions

1. Use examples to explain the metaphor "culture values".
2. Can you use examples to explain culture values in international business?

2. Hofstede's Five Value Dimensions
霍夫斯泰德的文化五维度

It is sometimes amazing for those who work in international business how different people in other cultures behave. We tend to have a human instinct that all people are the same—but they are not. Therefore, if we go to another country and make decisions based on how we operate in our own country, the chances we have will make some poor decisions. Geert Hofstede's research gives us insights into other cultures so that we can be more effective when interacting with people in other countries (董晓波，2013).

Geert Hofstede is an international authority on interculture social psychology. He analyzed a large database of employee values scores collected by IBM between 1967 and 1973 covering more than 70 countries, from which he first used the 40 largest countries only, and afterward extended the analysis to 50 countries and 3 regions. Scores were listed for 74 countries and regions, partly based on replications and extensions of the IBM study on different international populations in the editions of his work since 2001. Subsequent studies validating the earlier results have included civil service managers in 14 countries, commercial airline pilots and students in 23 countries, "up-market" consumers in 15 countries and "elites" in 19 countries. From the initial results and later additions, Hofstede developed a model that identifies five primary dimensions for differentiating cultures: power distance, individualism versus collectivism, masculinity versus femininity, uncertainty avoidance, and long-term versus short-term orientation. The value survey model has been widely discussed in international management literature and it appears to provide information of relevance in a managerial point of view (董晓波，2013).

2.1 Power Distance 权利距离

Power distance means the extent to which the less powerful members of institutions and organizations within a country, expect and accept that power is distributed unequally. It is the distance between the superior and the subordinate. It just shows how many subordinates can consent or dissent with their superiors. Among most oriental corporate cultures, hierarchism, greater centralization, are sometimes called "power-oriented culture" due to historical reasons. The superiors make the decision and are entitled more privileges. Their decisions and supervision are always positively evaluated by subordinates. In this situation, it does not matter if subordinates have a disagreement with their managers, especially in China, Japan and India (董晓波，2013).

In China and some other Asian countries, power distance is also associated with "the family culture". "Family culture at their least effective drains the energies and loyalties of subordinates to buoy up the leader." (魏家海，2000) In this kind of corporate culture the manager is like the "caring father" who knows better than his subordinates what is suitable for them and what should be done. The subordinates always esteem the managers because of their position and experience. There have both positive and negative aspects in the family cultures. It is just an easy managing system. But sometimes it is hard to get young creative employees work well because of the hierarchy (董晓波，2013).

Small Power Distance Culture

Small power distance culture values horizontal relationships where everyone is on a level playing field. Status symbols and privilege invite ridicule, and those who would set themselves above others are cut down to size. While a boss has power and authority, he must share the benefits of that power whenever possible and be careful to respect workers. Everyone is expected to have a voice in decision-making. Each person or group has rights and freedom to complain when those rights are violated. There is a strong sense of what is fair, and when workers sense they are being treated unfairly, they can complain and negotiate to improve their situations (董晓波，2013).

Hofstede found countries, like New Zealand, the United States, Australia, Denmark, and Finland enjoy small power distance culture. In these cultures, employees are not expected to rigidly conform to authority, and people have a certain latitude for disagreement. Superiors and subordinates feel relatively comfortable with shared decision-making and decentralization.

Small power distance countries hold the opinion that inequality in society should be minimized. People in these cultures believe that they should have access to power. To them, a hierarchy is an inequality of roles established for convenience. Subordinates consider superiors to be the same kind of people as they are, and superiors perceive their subordinates the same way. People in great power, such as supervisors or government officials, often interact with their constituents and try to look less powerful than they really are. In small power distance societies, the emphasis is on impersonal "truth" that can be obtained by any competent person. Small power distance culture is characterized by the following (董晓波，2013):

● Americans become uncomfortable when faced with the type of ceremony, tradition, and formalized social rules which are found more widely throughout Europe. They assume that informality is a prerequisite for sincerity. Moreover, they are likely to feel uneasy when others treat them with too much deference.

● Delighted with informal behavior. Americans generally take considerable delight when those in particularly high or powerful positions behave just like the everyday person on the street.

● Authority figures, such as professors, priests and supervisors, are often called by their first name rather than their official titles and last names.

● In many egalitarian societies, informality (for example, deemphasizing status differences) is reflected in the structure of everyday language. The distinction between the formal and informal you found in such languages as German and French, requires speakers to make linguistic choices that reflect the social status of the people being addressed. In contrast, English language makes no such distinctions.

● Authority figures, such as supervisors or college professors, are allowed to admit that they don't have all the answers. Also, they will not lose respect because of mistakes.

Large Power Distance Culture

Large power distance culture emphasizes the unequal distribution of power in institutions and organizations in a hierarchy of privilege. Power is experienced as a personal attribute, something to be felt rather than enforced. A few people have a lot of power; the vast majority has little. Members of large power distance culture will usually be quiet, soft-spoken, and polite, whether they are powerful individuals or not. People of large power distance culture will show their trust in you by asking for help and direction and will show their respect by remaining formal and lowering their eyes. And if they feel that you are being unfriendly or uncaring, they will be silent. Hofstede found that countries, such as Malaysia, Republic of Korea, China, Mexico, Indonesia, Pakistan, India and Japan, enjoy large power distance culture. In these societies, people respect formal hierarchical authority, and employees seldom violate chains of command or openly question decisions by their superiors.

In large power distance societies, communication is traditionally superior-centered. The superiors initiate all communications, outline the path of progress and the subordinates should follow. The superiors are never publicly criticized or contradicted.

2.2 Individualism versus Collectivism 个体主义和集体主义

Hofstede defines the second dimension as "Individualism pertains to societies in which the ties between individuals are loose: Everyone is expected to look after himself or herself and his or her immediate family. Collectivism as its opposite pertains to societies, in which people from birth are integrated into strong, cohesive groups, which throughout people's lifetime continue to protect them in exchange for unquestioning loyalty."

Individualism prefers self-sufficiency while collectivists give more recognition to their interdependent roles and obligations to the group. Studies of social categorization and intergroup relations show that people use salient characteristics as the basis to "group" others. The group is called the "in group" and other groups are called "out groups". The importance of the distinction is much greater for people from collectivism culture, and people from all types of culture categorize others in this way. Whereas individualistic societies are loosely knit, collectivist societies are composed of tight networks in which people operate as members of in groups and out groups, expecting to look after other members of their group in need and expect their group to look after them.

Individualistic Culture

Individualistic culture believes that people are supposed to take care of themselves and remain emotionally independent of groups, organizations or other collectives. Self-emphasis is important, even in budding friendships. Individuals can do whatever they want, and their "freedom" and their "rights" are of necessary values. They build contracts to protect their rights from others and to protect their dignity. Their high level of self-respect does not keep them from enjoying a good time and an occasional adventure, even if they might feel guilty later. When they are with friends, they are very open, but they can be very critical toward enemies. Individuals like to debate but will withdraw and become defensive with somebody they don't trust. They judge others by how much they need them. When they are interested, they can be loud with lots of questions but they are likely to look away when they get bored. Individuals are major units of social perception.

In the United States, emphasis on individuality can be seen in Americans' love for the automobile. Most Americans is capable of traveling in any direction at any time, expressing their individuality by becoming fully mobile, rather than being dependent on the schedules and routes of public transportation facilities.

Collectivist Culture

Collectivists value harmony and avoid directing confrontation. They emphasize building relationships with others through rituals and politeness, and task accomplishment becomes an indirect or secondary goal. Each individual represents the group to which he belongs to, so if an individual is hurt, the group is hurt; if an individual is helped, the group is helped; if an individual is shamed, the group is shamed. The communication style is typically indirect (Michael Argyle, 1984).

Asian, Latin American and West African nations are societies low in individualism but high in collectivism. In these societies, people would likely endorse group harmony, social order, and conformity in group relationships, deference to group forms, family relationships, loyalty, and consensus of viewpoints.

2.3 Masculinity versus Femininity 刚性文化和柔性文化

This dimension refers to the distribution of roles between the genders which is another fundamental issue for any society to which a range of solutions are found. The IBM studies revealed that (a) women's values differ less among societies than men's values; (b) men's values from one country to another contain a dimension from very assertive and competitive and maximally different from women's values on the one side, to modest and caring and similar to women's values on the other. The women in feminine countries have the same modest, caring values as the men; in the masculine countries they are somewhat assertive and competitive, but not as much as the men, so that these countries show a gap between men's values and women's values. The assertive pole has been called "masculine" and the modest, caring pole "feminine".

Masculine Culture

In high masculinity societies, people tend to believe that matters of material comfort, social privilege, status and prestige, access to power and influence and ability to consume are related to ability and that with enough opportunity any individual who wants these benefits of society can have them. High masculinity societies tend to reward financial and material achievements with preferential social prestige and status, and to attribute strong character and spiritual values to such high achievers.

In societies labeled masculine, such as Austria, Mexico, Japan, and Argentina, men are expected to hold the primary jobs and women are expected to remain at home and raise families. Female children are relegated to supporting roles, while male offspring are groomed for work roles and higher education.

Feminine Culture

In feminine societies, men and women are considered socially equal. Homosexuality is not a threat. Love and tenderness are for men and women alike. Intimate relationships without sex are allowed. Children need love, and parents should spend much time with them.

So-called feminine societies include all the Scandinavian countries, Portugal, Spain and several Pan-American nations. In these cultures, women are more prominent in management and professional fields. Organizations accommodate women's needs for maternity leave and childcare, and working environments tend to be less assertive and stressful.

2.4 Uncertainty Avoidance 不确定性规避

According to Hofstede, uncertainty avoidance refers to the lack of tolerance for ambiguity and uncertainty and the need for formal rules and high-level organizational structure. Nevertheless, cultures differ in the degree to which they can cope with uncertainties, tolerate ambiguity and adapt to the future. The unpredictability of the future and the resultant anxiety that this produces are part of the human experience. Hofstede's uncertainty-avoidance measure indicates the extent to which a culture conditions its members to feel either comfortable or uncomfortable in unstructured, ambiguous and unpredictable situations.

In cultures with high uncertainty avoidance, emotions are displayed in the way that everything is dangerous. They resist changes and worry about future. They are open for new things and changes. They don't have feelings of uncertainty about future.

Low Uncertainty Avoidance

Cultures of low uncertainty avoidance have more tolerance for a variety of opinions and have less concerns about ambiguity and uncertainty. This is reflected in a society that is less rule-oriented, more readily accepts changes and takes more and greater risks.

Societies with dualistic social philosophies or multidimensional religions place little value on any absolute truth. Instead, these "uncertainty-accepting" cultures practice religious and social organizations. Canada, Great Britain, the United States and several African nations are examples of such societies. Company practices in these societies tend toward an informal model relative to societies with highly structured environments, and they associate comparatively little ceremony with meetings and company rituals (王维波、车丽娟，2013).

High Uncertainty Avoidance

Cultures of high uncertainty avoidance have a low tolerance for uncertainty and ambiguity. This creates a rule-oriented society that institutes laws, rules, regulations and controls in order to reduce the amount of uncertainty.

Societies set up laws and rules to prevent uncertainty. In companies, duties and rights (internal and external) are controlled by authorities. Some cultures tend to have strong uncertain avoidance like France. In France many strict regulations are used and tasks are heavily centralized in companies. There will be a much higher demand for details when creating a contract. This is to avoid circumstance which could cause any kind of uncertainty. Organizing is therefore rather inflexible concerning changes which occur in business life (王维波、车丽娟，2013).

2.5 Long-term versus Short-term Orientation 长期取向和短期取向

This dimension describes a society's "time horizon" or the importance attached to the future versus the past and present. Long-term orientation stands for fostering of virtues oriented towards future rewards, in particular, perseverance and thrift. Its opposite pole, short-term orientation stands for fostering of virtues related to the past and present, in particular, respect for tradition, preservation of "face" and fulfilling socializing obligations (Hofstede, 2008).

Long-term Orientation

In long-term oriented societies, people value actions and attitudes that affect the future: persistence/perseverance, thrift and shame (王维波、车丽娟，2013). Steadfastness is valued and traditions are kept and honored. This value puts its focus on the future and involves a delay in short-term success to achieve long-term success. The emphasis is on long-term growth, perseverance and persistence. Important characteristics include modest, emphasis on obligation and virtues, thrift seen as a positive value.

Short-term Orientation

In short-term oriented societies, people value actions and attitudes that are affected by the present or the past: the normative statements, immediate stability, protecting one's own face, respect for tradition, and reciprocation of greetings, favors, and gifts (王维波、车丽娟，2013). Societies with short-term orientation tend to place the onus on truth and consistency. It includes delivering short-term success and putting the burden on the present instead of in the future. The emphasis is on quick and fast results. Important characteristics include emphasis on rights and values, strong convictions.

Societies who score low on this dimension, for example, prefer to maintain time-honored traditions and norms while viewing societal change with suspicion. Every society has to maintain some links with its own past while dealing with the challenges of the present and the future. Those cultures which score high on this dimension, on the other hand, take a more pragmatic approach: they encourage thrift and efforts in modern education as a way to prepare for the future (Hofstede G. J., 2005).

Key Term

Geert Hofstede 吉尔特·霍夫斯泰德

霍夫斯泰德，1928年生于荷兰，社会人文学博士，曾主管过IBM欧洲分公司的人事调查工作，是荷兰马斯特里赫特（Maastricht）大学国际管理系名誉教授，先后在欧洲多所大学任教，并担任香港大学荣誉教授，从事组织机构人类学和国际管理（Organizational Anthropology and International Management）方面的研究。

Glossary

subsequent	*adj.* 后续的
validating	*n./ adj.* 验证

commercial	*adj.* 商业的
dimension	*n.* 尺寸；程度
subordinate	*n.* 下属；部属
hierarchism	*n.* 等级主义

Comprehension Questions

1. Define Hofstede's five value dimensions.
2. Please list several countries where men are expected to hold the primary jobs and women are expected to remain at home and raise families.

3. Kluckhohn and Strodtbeck's Value Orientations
克拉克洪—斯托特柏克价值取向

Kluckhohn and Strodtbeck's theories are important and monumental in intercultural values research. It differentiates cultures through specific emphasis placed on different orientations. Their theories are influential and widely-applied because it attempts to create a universal value framework for all the cultures. Because of its significance and validity mentioned above, Kluckhohn and Strodtbeck's value orientations are widely applied in practice.

After examining hundreds of cultures, Kluckhohn and Strodtbeck have the conclusion that people turn to their cultures for answers especially on the following five questions: (1) What is the character of human nature? (2) What is the relation between human being and nature? (3) What is the orientation toward time? (4) What is the value placed on activity? (5) What is the relationship between ourselves and others? Of course, people in different cultures answer these five questions differently because they have unique value systems and cultural patterns. In the following passage, each of them will be in detail discussed (王维波、车丽娟，2013).

The first one is the character of human nature. When discussing human nature, we often encounter the questions of goodness and badness. As long as humans have self-consciousness, people have to put forward questions about good and evil. People cannot seek to control the actions of their members with institutions ranging from the religious to the political because cultures have the premise that people are instinctively evil. Most Christianity cultures belong to this pattern since Christians believe that humans have original sin given by Adam and Eve. The middle of continuum of this question is the orientation that people can be the mixture of evil and good. Which one they will inclined to depends on what happens in their lives; for instance, learning and good education can enlighten human beings (王维波、车丽娟，2013).

The relationship of humankind to nature is the second question that concerned about. Different answers for this question will result in different desires, attitudes and behaviors. Human beings are subjected to nature. The most powerful force of life is totally out of human beings' control, and people have to learn to accept it are the orientations that most cultures agree with. Cultures in the middle of the continuum think that people should live in harmony with nature in every possible way. In other words, people should cooperate with nature. The end of this one is that our human beings should conquer and manipulate the forces of nature with their advantages. A lot of Western countries are of this orientation.

Time orientation is the next one. Cultures vary widely in the concept of time. Past, present, future and how they influence interaction are the different values. The significance of prior events, or history are what past-orientated cultures emphasize. Traditions and established things are very important for people of this culture. They believe that past should be the guide for them to make decisions. We can see this orientation in China. China has a long and resplendent history, and most people respect the past very much. Children in China are happy to pretend to be the Monkey King, the supernatural hero of a medieval epic when there were plays.

Activity orientation is the fourth of Kluchhohn and Strodtbeck's value orientations. The orientation is "the way a culture views activity". They thought that being, being-in-becoming and doing are the common modes of activity expression. In being-oriented cultures, people have the view that the current activity is the one that matters the most. They believe that the act of "being" is one of the main goals and joys of life (王维波、车丽娟，2013).

The relational orientation is the final pattern of the five, which is about the ways in which people perceive their relationships with others. We can see that this kind of orientation ranging from authoritarianism to individualism in the following table. Many cultures only have authoritarian leaders and people of such culture believe that kind of social relationship to be the norm. Group is the most important of all society in collective cultures. Group and its affiliations have priority over individual's desires and goals. People think that "human are created equal" and therefore all people should have equal rights to control their fate totally by themselves in individual cultures.

Kluckhohn and Strodtbeck's five value orientations above can be summed up in the following table (王维波、车丽娟，2013):

Table 2-1　　　　Five Value Orientations

Orientation	Values and Behaviors		
Human Nature	Basically Evil	Mixture of Good and Evil	Basically Good
Relationship of Humankind to Nature	People Subject to Nature	People in Harmony with Nature	People the Master of Nature
Sense of Time	Past Orientated	Present Orientated	Future Orientated
Activity	Being	Being-in-Becoming	Doing
Social Relationship	Authoritarianism	Group-Orientated	Individualism

Values are at the core of the culture, which direct people's speech, choices and behavioral patterns. Therefore, the perceptions of love and marriage are often influenced by values. "Of all the problems discussed or studied in inter-culture communication research, value is one of the most important problems and deserves great attention." (Samovar, 1981) Kluckhohn and Strodtbeck introduced the concept of value orientations to study the relationship between culture values and communication behaviors more systematically. According to them, value orientations are the means by which society uses to solve the universal problems of daily life. With the process of "informatization", we could see great changes, including value changes on all levels. That means any change in the field of love and marriage must be derived from the changes of people's values about them (Kluckhohn, F. R. & Strodtbeck, F. L., 1961).

Key Terms

1. Kluckhohn and Strodtbeck Framework 克拉克洪—斯托特柏克构架

在分析文化差异时，我们引用最多的方法之一就是克拉克洪—斯托特柏克的构架。这一构架确定了 5 项基本的文化维度：人的本质、与环境的关系、时间取向、活动取向和社会关系。

2. culture communication 文化传播

文化传播是指文化从一个社会传到另一个社会，从一个区域传到另一个区域，以及从一个群体传到另一个群体的互动现象。党的二十大提出，坚守中华文化立场，提炼展示中华文明的精神标识和文化精髓，加快构建中国话语和中国叙事体系，讲好中国故事、传播好中国声音，展现可信、可爱、可敬的中国形象。加强国际传播能力建设，全面提升国际传播效能，形成同我国综合国力和国际地位相匹配的国际话语权。深化文明交流互鉴，推动中华文化更好走向世界。

Glossary

perception	*n.*	观念；洞察力
expatiate	*v.*	详述；细说；漫游
dimension	*n.*	尺寸；容积
handicraft	*n.*	手工艺品；技巧
context	*n.*	上下文；环境
affiliation	*n.*	联系；加入
authoritarian	*adj.*	权力主义的；独裁主义的
resplendent	*adj.*	灿烂的
medieval	*adj.*	中世纪的
thrive	*v.*	兴旺；繁荣；茁壮成长

Comprehension Questions

1. How do you define Kluckhohn and Strodtbeck's five value orientations?
2. What is the value placed on activity?

4. Edward T. Hall's High and Low Context
爱德华·霍尔的高语境和低语境

Another important aspect of communication in different cultures is the level of context in which the message is passed. Anthropologists and linguists use the terms "high" and "low" context (popularized by Edward Hall) to refer to the fact that when people communicate. They take for granted how much the listener knows about the subject under discussion. Societies or groups where people have close connections over a long period of time prefer high context. Many aspects of cultural behavior are not made explicit because most members know what to do and what to think from years of interaction with each other. Therefore, most of the information is in the physical context or is internalized in the people who are a part of the interaction in high-context cultures. Very little information is actually coded in the verbal message. For example, your family is probably an example of a high context environment. Low context, on the contrary, it refers to societies where people tend to have many connections but of shorter duration or for some specific reasons. In these societies, cultural behavior and beliefs may need to be spelled out explicitly so that those coming into the cultural environment know how to behave. Accordingly, most of the information is contained in the verbal message, and very little is embedded in the context or within the participants in low-context cultures (董晓波，2013).

The high-context culture and low-context culture are the terms that refer to "the fact that when people communicate, they take for granted how much the listener knows about the subject under discussion. In low-context communication, the listener knows very little and must be told practically everything. However, in high-context communication the listener is already 'contexted' and so does not need to be given much background information."

Let's look at the following case for a better understanding of how high-context culture and low-context culture work in our daily life. One day, an American businessman, together with one of his Chinese friends went to visit a Chinese family. In the living room, the American was much attracted by the Chinese handicrafts on the shelves. He pointed to one of the handicrafts and extolled it particularly. The Chinese host immediately took the handicraft out of the shelf and gave it to the American and said, "Take it as a present." The American was surprised. He refused to take it and said, "I didn't mean it. It is a precious handicraft." But the Chinese host did not stop offering until the American took it. Looking at the handicraft in his hand, he felt embarrassed. The next day, the American businessman explained to his Chinese friend: "I did not have any intention to have the handicraft. I complimented the host on the handicraft just because it is good. I meant nothing else at all." (董晓波，2013)

From this example, we can find that people of different cultural backgrounds usually behave and respond in different ways in the same context. To be exact, people of high-context culture and low-context culture may sometimes suffer from culture shock in their cross-culture communication. To the Chinese host, extolling the handicraft implies wanting it, as there is a saying in Chinese: When you listen to someone's talk, you must judge by his tone. The tone of the American's compliments told the Chinese host that the American liked the handicraft implies nothing but his personal comments on it or politeness. The result of their communication made both of them a little embarrassed.

Why are the people of different cultural backgrounds so different in such a context? Let's see more explanation given by Edward T. Hall, an American anthropologist. In Edward T. Hall's theory of high-context culture and low-context culture, he believes that any cultural transaction can basically be divided into two communication systems: high-context and low-context. In high-context transmission of message, only minimal information is in the transmitted message (explicated code), while most of the information is in the physical world or in individuals. By contrast, most of the information is in the transmitted message in low-context transmission.

The cultures in this world can be classified into two major categories: high-context and low-context cultures basing on these kinds of different contexts. In high-context culture, the members usually have the same language of some race as well as the same norms of values, so information is easy to transmit; while in low-context culture, it is different because various differences exist in the society, resulting from the presence of many subcultures independent of each other (董晓波，2013).

Although no culture exists exclusively at either extreme, in general, low-context cultures refer to groups of cultures that value individual orientation and overt communication codes and maintain a heterogeneous normative structure with low cultural demand characteristics. Conversely, high-context cultures refer to groups of cultures that value group identity orientation and covert communication codes and maintain a homogeneous normative structure with high cultural demand characteristics. In general, Germany, Scandinavian countries and the US are situated at the low-context end of the continuum; Chinese, Japanese and Korean cultures are located at the high-context end. It is obvious that communication can be influenced by philosophy. Confucianism, for example, has permeated the culture of all the three Eastern Asian countries, and it influences the way people communicate.

In high-context culture of China, for example, a large portion of the message is left unspecified and needs to be accessed through the context, nonverbal cues, between-the-lines interpretation of what is actually said or written, and which is reflected by frequent using of uncompleted sentences. In contrast, in North America, which is labeled as a low-context culture, messages are expected to be explicit and specific. More is spelt out than left for the receiver to deduce from the context.

French contracts are usually about ten times shorter than American contracts. Americans like to have a lot of the context stated explicitly. The French don't care very much about the explanation, as much of the information is taken for granted (董晓波，2013).

In high-context cultures, what people mean is judged not only by their words but also by the context in which the message occurs. In such a context, "yes" can't necessarily mean "yes" but probably means "no". But in low-context culture, people judge what others mean mainly by their words. In such a context, "yes" usually means "yes". Let's look back at the case given at the beginning. Culturally speaking, both the Chinese host and the American businessman are right in the context. Because of the high-context culture, the Chinese host judged what the American businessman said by the tone of his words, so he offered him the handicraft. Because of his low-context culture, the American meant only what he said and no more other connotations.

High-context cultures, in which both the sender and the receiver can well understand the context and use the context to communicate the message. Members of these cultures rely on context to help clarify and complete the message. Members of low-context cultures, however, put their thoughts into words. They tend to think that if thoughts are not solidified in words, they will not be understood correctly or completely.

Yet, a Westerner can easily suppose the situation in reverse. An American traveler to Beijing gets off the plane after 24 hours of continuous travel and in response to the same comment, "You must be tired!" replied, "Tired! I've never been so tired in my life. I've been sitting on planes or in waiting rooms for 24 hours and wondered if my legs would work again! My eyes are so gritty with sleep."

The following part may help you better understand high-context culture and low-context culture (Edward T. Hall, 1961).

Characteristics of High-context Culture

1. Long-term relationships.
2. People almost enjoy the same norms or values.
3. Strong boundaries—who is accepted as belonging vs. who is considered an "outsider".
4. Dense, intersecting networks and long-term relationships, strong boundaries, relationships more important than tasks.
5. Most of the information is in the physical world or in individuals.
6. Knowledge is situational and relational.
7. People value group identity orientation and covert communication codes and maintain a homogeneous normative structure with high cultural demand characteristics.
8. Decisions and activities focus around personal face-to-face relationships, and often around a central person who has authority.
9. A large portion of the message is left unspecified and needs to be accessed through the context.
10. People judge what someone is talking about not only by what he is saying but also by the context in which the message occurs.
11. More knowledge is below the waterline—implicit, patterns that are not fully conscious, hard to explain even if you are a member of that culture (董晓波，2013).

Characteristics of Low-context Culture

1. More interpersonal connections of shorter duration.
2. People enjoy different subcultures.
3. Loose, wide networks, shorter term, compartmentalized relationships, task more important than relationship.
4. Most of the information is in the transmitted message.
5. People value individual orientation and overt communication codes and maintain a heterogeneous normative structure with low cultural demand characteristics.
6. Messages are expected to be explicit and specific.
7. People judge what someone is talking about mainly by what he is saying.
8. Knowledge is more often transferable.
9. Task-centered. Decisions and activities focus around what needs to be done, division of responsibilities.
10. More knowledge is above the waterline—explicit, consciously organized (董晓波, 2013).

Although we tend to categorize cultures as being either high-context or low-context, context is a cultural dimension that ranges from high to low.

Key Terms

1. high context and low context 高语境和低语境

语境是使用语言的环境，包括一切主客观因素。美国文化人类学家爱德华·T. 霍尔在 1976 年出版的《超越文化》一书中，提出文化具有语境性，并将语境分为高语境（High Context，即 HC）和低语境（Low Context，即 LC）。霍尔认为：“任何事物均可被赋予高、中、低语境的特征。”

2. Scandinavia 斯堪的纳维亚

斯堪的纳维亚亦指斯堪的纳维亚半岛（Scandinavia peninsula），位于欧洲西北部地区，主要包括挪威、瑞典、丹麦等国家。这些国家虽然政治互相独立，但共同的称谓显示了他们的文化和历史有深厚的渊源。“斯堪的纳维亚”一词对于世界各地的人有不同的含义。

Glossary

interpersonal	*adj.*	人际间的
heterogeneous	*adj.*	异种的
transfer	*v.*	转移；迁移
waterline	*n.*	吃水线
exclaim	*v.*	大叫；呼喊
categorize	*v.*	分类
transmission	*n.*	传播；传送
nonverbal	*adj.*	非言辞的；不用语言的
boundary	*n.*	边界；分界线

Comprehension Questions

1. What are the characteristics of the high-context culture?
2. In what context "yes" can mean "yes" but probably mean "no"?

Extended Activities

Case Analysis

Case 1

Liu Zhong, the President of a Chinese firm, told a story on a radio program of how he once almost lost a valuable American employee working for him in New York. He emailed every day to the American, inquiring for the index number he was most concerned about. To his great astonishment, his American employee turned in his resignation after a week. Liu Zhong was puzzled how the employee could do that to him. He had given such great attention to the employee's job. A Chinese employee would have been more than happy if his or her boss had showed such great concern for him or her. He then found out that, unlike Chinese employees, the American took what meant great concern to Chinese as distrust. But Liu Zhong assumed unconsciously that the American was more similar to his Chinese employees than he actually was and treated him just as he treated any Chinese employee.

（Adapted from：魏家海. 东西文化价值观的两重性与跨文化交际［J］. 西安外国语学院学报，2000.）

Questions for Discussion

1. Why does the American employee turn in his resignation?
2. What kind of response may a Chinese employee have if a boss shows great concern for him or her?
3. What are the reasons of this communication barrier?

Case 2

Exchanging for some Country A controlled land in Country B, Country B's government agreed to build up a new facility at another military installation controlled by Country A's army. After the preliminary drawings were completed, a conference was held with the two states' engineers and one translator repeated questions in Country A's language; the Country A's questions were then translated back into Country B's language.

A Country A's engineer asked a question about the maximum distance allowed between two points that he had indicated in the drawing. The question was translated, and a Country B's engineer quickly raised his hand with his index finger pointing upward and answered "one meter". The translator, thinking no translation was necessary, remained silent. The Country B's engineers wrote two meters in their notes; the Country A's engineer wrote one meter. (In Country B, when using fingers to show a number, begin counting with the thumb as number one; therefore, the index finger, being the second finger from the thumb, represents the number two.)

（Adapted from：魏家海. 东西文化价值观的两重性与跨文化交际［J］. 西安外国语学院学报，2000.）

Questions for Discussion

1. Why did the translator think no translation was necessary when Country A's engineer answered "one meter"?
2. Does the index finger represent the same number in Country A and Country B?
3. Can you use this example to explain that encoding and decoding are the areas where miscommunication takes place?

Activities

Task 1

Insert the phrase "intercultural communication" into a search engine on the Internet and report to your group what you can find out about the studies of intercultural communication both at home and abroad.

Task 2

Clip a story from the local newspaper that is related to some aspect of intercultural communication such as problems encountered by persons of other cultures in the acculturation process or problems between subgroups; give a short report to the class.

Task 3

Write a one-page proposal for improving relationships between US students and students from other cultures in your school.

Task 4

In small groups, play a word-association game. Your instructor will compose a list of potentially culture-bound words such as motherland, freedom, etc., and then say the words once at a time. Write down the first thing that comes into your mind as you hear each word. Compare your reactions. Are there any major differences within the group? Discuss them. Then compare your answers with the entire class and discuss.

Further Reading

Confucius and Confucianism

Confucius (551 B.C.—479 B.C.), an intellectual like the Greek philosopher Socrates, was the founder of Confucianism. He was known for his wit and great wisdom. Confucius was one of the greatest thinkers and educators in the history of China, and his legacy lies in the following three aspects. Firstly, Confucius and his disciples compiled and preserved literary works of the generations. Secondly, Confucius established a philosophy (a system of philosophical thoughts) with "Ren" as its fundamental virtue. Thirdly, Confucius founded a systematic educational framework.

Confucianism is not a religion but a set of practical principles and ethical rules for daily life.

Confucius was the founder of Confucian school. His doctrine covers various areas, with ritual and "Ren" (benevolence) as its central concerns. His followers, who regularly surrounded him and recorded his teachings in oral or written form, provided us with what we now know of his ideas.

Confucius intended ideally to set up a moral system to govern all relationships in all the three levels of family, community and state. Confucius argued that society was made up of five relationships: those between ruler and subjects (the relation of righteousness), husband and wife (chaste conduct), father and son (love), elder brother and younger brother (order), and between friends (faithfulness). Each of these relationships presumes the existence and legitimacy of a social hierarchy requires. People with higher-status must provide protection and consideration, while those with lower-status owe respect and obedience.

Out of five relations, three occur within the family. The regulation factors in family relationships are extended to the whole community and state. The top virtue is filial piety, which demands that the son honors and respects his father and fulfills the demands of his elders.

Confucianism gives priority to duty, patriotism, selflessness, hard work, virtue and respect for hierarchy, both familial and societal. Teaching and learning are highly valued, moderation in all things is preferred, conspicuous consumption is frowned, losing one's temper is unacceptable, and persistence in solving difficult problems is widely valued. Since human being is born to be good in nature, it is the responsibility of each individual to train his or her moral character in the standards of behavior.

The collectivism values of Confucianism mandate a style of communication in which respecting the relationship through communication is very important. Group harmony, avoidance of loss of face to others and oneself, and a modest presentation of oneself are means of respecting the relationship. One does not say what one actually thinks when it might hurt others in the group.

Confucianism plays an important role in Chinese culture. It is suggested to hold a critical attitude to inherit and assimilate the fine elements of our national culture. With the trend of globalization, it is a realistic and wise alternative to push the Chinese culture into the culture of the world (魏家海，2007).

Unit 3 Managing Intercultural Conflicts

Learning Objectives

After learning this unit, you will be able to:

- ✧ define intercultural conflicts;
- ✧ describe culture shock;
- ✧ understand the importance of intercultural conflicts and culture shock.

Warm-up

1. What is your first feeling about culture shock?
2. Use some examples to explain intercultural conflicts.

Focused Study

1. Intercultural Conflicts 跨文化冲突

According to Martin and Nakayama (2005), "Conflict is usually defined as involving a perceived or real incompatibility of goals, values, expectations, processes, or outcomes between two or more interdependent individuals or groups." We can be sure that conflicts are unavoidable. As they always have, conflicts are happening all around the world. Thus cultural conflicts are the conflicts occurring in intercultural communication which are caused by cultural differences that can also not be avoided.

The clashes between the American values of individualism, directness and time consciousness, and the Japanese interests in face-to-face discussion and consensus building are the differing values of task-oriented versus process-oriented cultures. Americans come to business meetings well informed, focused and expect an open dialogue. They are willing to take action and assign responsibilities. Their Japanese partners place more emphasis on group harmony, consensus and the need to discuss proposals and actions—they rarely make an immediate decision.

With three sets of competing values—American, Japanese and Indonesian—gaining momentum, cultural clash can intensify. And teamwork can be seriously damaged once cultural problems cause interpersonal clashes. The culture shock, the generic intercultural stress, is a result of such an intercultural encounter. It requires that the individual adjusts at least temporarily to regain equilibrium and cope with the new situation. This requires the suspension of certain behavior, and possibly norms and values and basic assumptions, and the accommodation of new behavior and adaptation of norms, values and basic assumptions to accommodate those new ways. This may meet with conscious or unconscious resistance of the individual to adapt initially. This causes additional stress.

Cultural differences often command much more attention than similarities. These differences are often caused by ignorance or lack of patience to appear insurmountable or even lead to intolerable "culture clash". This clash and lack of patience are the very evident in the movie *Pushing Hands* by director Ang Lee. A white mainstream American woman, Martha, marries a first generation Chinese American, Alex Chu, and has a son. The family grows until one day the father of Alex Chu comes from the Chinese mainland to live with them. He speaks no English. Conflicts arise between the American wife and Chinese father-in-law immediately. There are distinct differences between Martha and Master Chu's cultures. They both have distinct beliefs concerning how people should act or behave in a society. The first spoken sound in the movie comes from Martha when she yells at Master Chu for placing metal in the microwave. Master Chu has probably never worked with a microwave and cannot communicate to ask about the proper procedure. This is the first main example of the cultural difference, lack of understanding and lack of knowledge. The lack of space is the other thing Martha also doesn't understand. Her husband again explains the Asian culture. He says that ten families would live in a home of their size in China.

New cultures force themselves upon Master Chu. He is forced to conform to the new culture around him in order to survive and be happy. He is forced to give up the idea in his old culture that the elders are supposed to be cared for by their children. He finds his way to Chinatown to escape further clashes between his daughter-in-law and himself in his son's home. There he finds even in Chinatown the Asian culture has been forced to conform to mainstream American culture. Respect for elders has been disregarded. Everything has become a business.

People are forced by new culture to conform in order to survive. Master Chu has no choice but to become American in many ways. He must learn to use microwaves, learn new ways of behaving and must understand his new American culture.

Key Terms

1. *Pushing Hands*《推手》

《推手》是一部由李安执导的剧情类电影，由郎雄、王莱等主演。该片于 1991 年 12 月 7 日上映。该片讲述了朱老退休后被接到了美国，由于语言不通，生活习惯不同，爆发家庭矛盾后，对祖国无限思念的故事。

2. dialogue 对话

对话，指两个或更多的人用语言交谈。对话是不同文化之间进行沟通的主要方式。在人类面临百年未有之大变局的形势下，需要以平等互利、相互尊重为基础，通过不同渠道和形式，开展更多的对话沟通和交流，以实现不同文化间的和谐共处。党的二十大提出，中国坚持对话协商，推动建设一个持久和平的世界；坚持共建共享，推动建设一个普遍安全的世界；坚持合作共赢，推动建设一个共同繁荣的世界；坚持交流互鉴，推动建设一个开放包容的世界；坚持绿色低碳，推动建设一个清洁美丽的世界。

Glossary

drawback	*n.* 缺点；不利条件
disintegration	*n.* 瓦解；衰变
conform	*v.* 使一致；遵从
initial	*adj.* 开始的；最初的
leap	*v.* 跳跃
intercourse	*v.* 交流；交往
frustration	*n.* 挫折；失败
assumption	*n.* 假定；设想
prop	*n.* 支持者
subsequent	*adj.* 随后的；后来的

Comprehension Questions

1. Use examples to explain the metaphor "intercultural conflicts".
2. Can you list several examples about "intercultural conflicts"?

2. Culture Shock 文化休克

2.1 Feeling of Culture Shock 文化休克感知

The term, culture shock, describes the anxiety produced when a person moves to a completely new environment, especially when a person arrives in a new country where he/she is confronted with a new cultural environment. This term expresses the lack of direction, the feeling of not knowing what to do or how to do things in a new environment, and not knowing what is appropriate or inappropriate.

The feeling of culture shock is generally set in after the first few weeks of coming to a new place. People suffer a lot at the very beginning, as they usually go through the following.

Familiar signs and symbols are lost. Generally speaking, culture shock is precipitated by the anxiety that results from losing all familiar signs and symbols of social intercourse. These signs are the thousand and one ways in which we orient ourselves to the situations of daily life: when to shake hands and what to say when we meet people, when and how to give tips, how to give orders to servants, how to accept and when to refuse invitations, when to take statements seriously and when not. People suffer little from these social activities when they are at home in their own country. However, when they are away in a foreign country, they are always at a loss for what to do and how to do it.

Familiar cues are removed. Suppose an individual enters a strange culture, all or most of the familiar cues are removed. He is like a fish out of water. No matter how broad-minded or good-willed he may be, a series of props have been knocked from him. This is followed by a feeling of frustration and anxiety. First they reject the environment which causes the discomfort: the ways of the host country are bad because they make us feel bad.

All cultures are not exactly the same. As most people take for granted that all cultures operate and behave probably in exactly the same manner as their own, they are "shocked" or made temporarily uncomfortable by the differences and unpredictability they encounter, whether it be in the language, food or various social situations of everyday life. One positive of the experience of living abroad is the ability to better understand one's own culture and society through observing other's.

While American culture may be more straightforward in manner and rules of behavior, Asian cultures are more ambiguous, or relate more to individual situations and cannot be easily understood by or explained to those born outside their culture. For instance, in Chinese culture a lot goes unsaid but is still completely understood by most, as for foreigner, this can leave them at a complete loss. Remember no matter what the differences are, we all have the same needs and desires even if we communicate them differently, which is quite crucial (Ping, H. & Zhang, G. Y., 1999).

An American business delegation came to China to sign a big contract with a Chinese company in order to enter the market in China. What was so warm is the host prepared an expensive welcome dinner: nice dishes of every kind, delicate food from land and sea. It was a banquet rather than a dinner. The delegation felt a little worried on the spot and was hesitant to sign the contract, for they thought such a company would not manage a business efficiently.

Both the American businesspeople and Chinese businesspeople suffered from culture shock in the case above, as the business communication came to an end due to the welcome dinner offered by the Chinese. Actually neither the Chinese nor Americans were wrong from the point of view of their own cultures. To the Chinese, they thought they did nothing wrong. They had to perform the duties of the host, as being warm and hospitable is a virtue which is valued by Chinese people in their traditional culture. To the Americans, as people are expected to focus more on business than on overelaborate formalities in their traditional culture, so they thought such a company would not run a business efficiently.

From the case above, we can be sure that it is a must for companies, especially the management staff, to well-understand the foreign culture in order to avoid culture shock and make good profits in their business with foreign companies (杨军红，2005).

2.2 Stages of Culture Shock 文化休克的阶段

Culture shock is frequently described as a series of stages that a person goes through. People will experience these stages when they are enjoying a culture different from their own in a new country. In the beginning what people will experience in the new environment make them excited; soon they feel disappointed by what they actually experienced; later on they try to understand what is going on around them and feel happy; then they begin to adjust themselves to the new environment and enjoy their new life; and finally they feel comfortable in the new environment, as comfortable as in their old culture. Their feelings change as they experience (董晓波，2013).

The Honeymoon Stage

The first stage is the incubation stage, which is also called the "honeymoon" stage, as everything encountered is new and exciting. At this stage, the new arrivals may feel euphoric and may be pleased by all of the new things encountered. Those who have just come to a foreign country are fascinated with everything that is new. They are embarking on a long sought-after adventure. People at this stage will demonstrate an eagerness to please people around, a spirit of cooperation and an active interest in listening to people speaking. The excitement of life in a new culture seems to be endless (王维波、车丽娟，2013).

In reality, it is delightful to get along with the new arrival, but due to their enthusiasm to please, they frequently nod or smile to indicate understanding when they don't understand at all in fact. When misunderstandings mount up, they are likely to experience the second stage of cultural adjustment (董晓波，2013).

The Hostility Stage

Afterward, the second stage presents itself. A person may encounter some difficult time and crises in daily life. For instance, people may suffer communication difficulties if not being understood.

In general, this stage is featured by frustration, anger, anxiety and sometimes depression. The initial excitement is taken place by frustration with the daily bureaucracy and the weariness of speaking and listening to another language every day. The new arrivals will be at a difficult, painful stage. They can be difficult to work with. They will try everyone's patience and quite possibly give up, if they do not share their feelings with someone and realize what is happening to them (王维波、车丽娟，2013).

A Chinese manager was sent to work in the United States for one year. As he couldn't bear what he encountered in the country, he returned home in three months. He couldn't enjoy the local food, the TV programs, or the ways of communicating with the local people. Because of his behaviors and poor English, he was even sometimes misunderstood by the local people (董晓波，2013).

The Recovery Stage

The third stage is characterized by gaining some understanding of the new culture. People will experience a new feeling of pleasure and sense of humor. One may start to feel a certain psychological balance. The new arrivals may not feel as lost as before and start to have a feeling of self-confidence. They are more familiar with the environment and want to identify themselves with it.

At this stage, the new arrivals start feeling more positive and they try to develop comprehension of everything they do not understand. The whole situation starts to become more favorable: they recover from the symptoms of the former stage, and adjust themselves to the new norms, values and beliefs and traditions of the new country. They begin to see that they can learn to appreciate.

This more relaxed state of being is accomplished by making some friends, being able to manage the size and complexity of the environment and understanding what is going on. They become generally easy to get along with because they are relaxed and receptive (王维波、车丽娟，2013).

The Adjustment Stage

At the fourth stage, people realize that the new culture has good and bad things to offer. This stage can be one of double integration or triple integration depending on the number of cultures that people have to go through. This integration is accompanied by a more solid feeling of belonging. People begin to make definition for themselves and establish goals for living.

At this stage, people have reached a point where they actually feel good because they are well-educated to understand the new culture. The things that initially made them feel uncomfortable or strange are now things that they understand. This acquisition of understanding alleviates much of the stress.

When people not only retain allegiance to their home culture, but also "feel at ease" with what they meet and where they are, they have successfully adjusted to the new culture, and should feel proud of themselves for achieving the ability to live successfully in two cultures (董晓波，2013).

The Biculturalism Stage

At this stage people have become comfortable in both old and new cultures. To some extent, they achieve biculturalism. Biculturalism is viewed by some as the healthy and even ideal stage of adaptation in which one's original cultural world view remains intact as alternative cultural frames are acquired. Though it is of controversy whether it is within people's reach to be really "bicultural" (王维波、车丽娟，2013).

The stages above take place at different periods and each person has his own way of dealing with the different stages of culture shock. Many factors contribute to the duration and effects of culture shock. For instance, the individual's state of mental health, type of personality, previous experiences, socioeconomic conditions, familiarity with the language family and social support systems, and level of education. As a consequence, some stage will be longer and more difficult to deal with than others (董晓波，2013).

2.3 Symptoms of Culture Shock 文化休克症状

The symptoms of culture shock mentioned above can be divided into two aspects: physically and psychologically.

Physical symptoms of culture shock. Some of the physical symptoms of culture shock include: too much sleep or too little sleep, eating too much or having no appetite, frequent minor illnesses, upset stomachaches or headaches and a general feeling of uneasiness.

A Chinese businessman was sent to work in the United States for a special project for one week. He suffered a lot for what he would eat every day. Sometimes he just went hungry as he didn't have any appetite for Western food. When it was time for meals, he was busy looking for Chinese food. One week later, he returned home exhausted and dispirited. When asked what he had missed most about home, he said, "Chinese food" (董晓波，2013).

Psychological symptoms of culture shock. Some of the psychological symptoms of culture shock include: loneliness or boredom, homesickness, idealizing home, feeling helpless and dependent, irritability and even hostility, social withdrawal, excessive concern for health or security, rebellion against rules and authority, feeling like you have no control over your life, feeling unimportant and being a foreigner, crying, negative stereotyping of people in the host country.

As we can see, many of these symptoms are usual. This is why it can be difficult to recognize when you are having culture shock. Not everyone will experience all of these symptoms and each person reacts differently. Let's study the following case and see how Professor Liu suffered from the symptoms of culture shock during his few days at a conference in the United States (董晓波，2013).

Liu, a Chinese professor of medical science, went to California to present a paper at an academic conference. He arrived expectant and happy and enjoyed his first days very much. At the conference, he felt quite confident in his area of research and was able to perform well in his presentation. But after a few days, he began to feel uncomfortable. He spoke very good English on medical science, but he had very different social interaction skills from the local people and he was unsure of the cues and the communication style. He became increasingly worried as he began misunderstanding simple English greetings and table conversation conventions. When someone greeted him with "Hi, how's it going?", he thought they had asked him "Where are you going?" and answered with the name of the conference hall, only to get a quizzical stare from them. At a Western style dinner, a colleague asked, "So how're you enjoying the States?" He thought he heard, "How are you enjoying your steak?" and answered that he was eating chicken, not beef. They smiled and patiently repeated the question and then both laughed at the error.

Such misunderstanding and miscommunications were minor. But for Professor Liu, he was beginning of a sense of "culture confusion". By the end of the conference, he felt a deep sense of "culture stress" and was worn out from having pay attention to so many new expressions and ways of dealing with things. He felt his handshake was not as firm as Americans', and found that people reacted unusually when he modestly insisted his English was not good after they complimented him, that he didn't know how to accept dinner invitations properly and therefore missed out on several lunches, and so on. In the end, he was so bewildered that he felt the full impact of "culture shock" (董晓波，2013).

2.4 Symptoms of Reverse Culture Shock 反向文化休克症状

It is also natural that some people suffer from culture shock even when they are in their own country. It is not an easy task to come home after spending some time abroad. A similar adjustment period and its accompanying symptoms usually occur when a sojourner returns home. This is often called reverse culture shock. It takes people by surprise when they don't realize that it is normal. In fact, it's somewhat ironic. The sojourner has been longing to return to the old, familiar culture of home. But once home, the returnees find many things to complain or criticize and often ask why the old culture can't be more like the one they recently encountered. Friends and family members often find the returnees impatient with things that never used to cause complaint. Returnees' most common complaint is that nobody wants to hear about the wonderful new experiences they have had (董晓波，2013).

Returnees find that people at home also have had new experiences to which they must adjust. For example, things have changed at the company where they work; people have been promoted, achieved success, retired, left for another employer and so forth. They are something of an outsider after returning "home" and may have a new job to get used to as well as new contacts to make. They feel they have been laboring in foreign fields for the sake of the corporation, usually at some (nonmonetary) cost and personal sacrifice, but upon returning often they feel they are not valued. In response to it, some companies provide mentors and training programs to ease reentry (董晓波，2013).

Businesspeople who return after years abroad often feel they suffer a lot on reverse culture shock than they had when adjusting to the other culture. It may be that an inverse relationship exists between ease of adjustment to an unfamiliar culture and degree of reverse culture shock: the easier it is to adjust to a new culture, the harder it is to readjust to home culture.

Let's see the following example and find out how Gerhard Baumgartner suffered reverse culture shock.

Gerhard Baumgartner, a German engineer, suffered from reverse culture shock when he returned home from the Middle East where he stayed for five years.

"When coming home after a five-year stay in the Middle East I was really happy at first. Although I loved being there, I really missed home a lot. And then it seemed so great to have all the things back that I have missed for so long. But a month later things seemed to get worse. I was very miserable, got depressed and missed the Middle East. The people appeared strange and even my family and friends, whom I have missed for so long, started to upset me." (Beamer, L., & Varner, I., 2005)

This type of reaction is unfortunately not uncommon; many expatriates face such situation when returning home. After a short while of being enthusiastic about being home again, they feel increasingly isolated and frustrated with their home environment. In fact, what is happening is a second culture shock.

As in the example the engineer is no longer really "German" and has become more "Middle East". So coming home is similar to coming to another culture. While living abroad many people lose the perspective on their culture. What they miss tends to be an idealized home. Once they move back, they get confronted with the reality (房玉清、姚颖，2014).

Key Term

biculturalism 二元文化

人类文化的二元结构是基于人类自身生物特性而形成的两种文化路向。在此，"文化"的定义应该理解为梁漱溟先生关于"文化"的定义，即所谓文化就是"人类生活的样法罢了"。就像生物世界的多样性，人类生存的样法也是多样的，最明显的是他看似对立的二元性。就像生物从无性繁殖到两性繁殖这个进步，人类的文化也是从单元结构走向二元结构，这是人类自然演化的进步。

Glossary

monetary	*adj.*	货币的；金融的
reverse	*v.*	逆转；倒退；改变
boredom	*n.*	无聊；厌烦
withdrawal	*n.*	撤退；退回；取消
insurmountable	*adj.*	无法解决的；难以对付的
seniority	*n.*	长辈；职位高
subtle	*adj.*	微妙的；不明显的
empathetic	*adj.*	移情作用的
dehydrate	*v.*	使脱水
ambiguity	*n.*	模棱两可；含糊不清

Questions for Discussion

1. What are the symptoms of culture shock?
2. How many stages are there during the period of culture shock? What are they?
3. Try to give some details of transition adjustments.

3. Effective Management 有效管理

3.1 Defense Mechanisms against Culture Shock 文化休克的预防机制

We have some defense mechanisms against culture shock in reality. To help us cope with the effects of culture shock, we devise some defense mechanisms as we are trying to adjust ourselves to a new culture.

Repression. The first coping mechanism is called "repression". When we pretend that everything is acceptable and that nothing bothers us, this happens.

Regression. The second one is called "regression". This occurs when we start to act as if we are younger than we actually are. We act like a child and we forget everything. Sometimes, we become careless and irresponsible.

Isolation. The third kind of defense mechanism is called "isolation". We would rather be home alone and we don't want to communicate with anybody. We try to avoid the effects of culture shock with isolation. Because it separates us from those things that could really help us, isolation is one of the worst coping mechanisms we can use.

Rejection. The last type of defense mechanism is called "rejection". We think we don't need anybody with this coping mechanism. We feel we are coping fine alone and we don't try to ask for help.

The defense mechanisms we utilize are not helpful as a matter of fact. Occasionally, if we only use one of these coping mechanisms to help ourselves survive, that is acceptable. We must be cautious with these coping mechanisms. Because they prevent us from making the necessary adjustments to the new culture, these mechanisms can really hurt us.

3.2 Alleviating Culture Shock 减轻文化休克

Frankly speaking, culture shock can be alleviated or minimized. By selecting employees for overseas assignments who possess certain personal and professional qualifications, some multinational firms try to minimize culture shock. In addition, it is advisable that the company conduct training programs for employees prior to an overseas assignment.

Culture shock is an unfortunate side effect of going abroad, but people need to know that it will pass. By learning about potential problems and differences, developing language skills, and making a plan to get involved in the new community, people will be able to effectively deal with the challenges of acculturation, alleviate or minimize culture shock. There are many ways for people to take for reducing cultural clashes actually. Here are some suggestions for enhancing the international business experience by reducing clashes with the local culture (董晓波，2013).

Learn throughout your stay. What you should understand is that learning about the host culture is a process that continues throughout your stay in the host culture and beyond. After your arrival in the host country, far more learning will occur. Make sure that you use a wide variety of information sources to learn about the host culture, including local people, libraries, newspapers, tourist information and your own observation. In order to learn as quickly as possible, you need to find a friend or colleague (either a local resident or an experienced expatriate).

Get involved. Become familiar with your immediate physical surroundings after your arrival. Leave your hotel and walk to a number of different directions, armed with a good map of the vicinity, exploring the city or town on foot. Identify local buildings, where they are in relation to one another, what they are used for, the pattern, if any, of how streets are configured, and where people seem to congregate. Learning about other aspects of the culture, a familiarity with the "lay of the land" will provide an excellent base.

Master simple tasks. Work on familiarizing yourself with some of the basic things within the first several days of arrival and everyday survival skills that your hosts take for granted. These include such capacities as using the local currency, using the telephone system and the public transportation system, buying stamps and ordering for a menu. You will minimize frustrations and embarrassments quickly by mastering these seemingly simple tasks, as well as gain the self-confidence to master some of the subtler aspects of the host culture.

Try to understand. Try to understand your hosts in terms of their culture rather than your own though it is difficult. Try to make sense of it in terms of their culture when you encounter a behavior or an attitude that appears strange or even offensive, rather than you own. This is not to suggest that you should adopt their attitudes or behaviors, or even like them, but when viewed from their proper cultural perspective, you will better understand them (林大津，2008).

Learn to live with ambiguity. Learn to live with the ambiguity of not having all the answers particularly in the beginning. Trying to operate in a new culture is, to a great extent, a highly ambiguous situation. The person who insists on having immediate and clear-cut answers for everything is likely to be frustrated. It is important for the cultural neophyte to know that there will be many unanswered questions. To eventually adjust to the new culture, try being patient and learning to live with ambiguity, the new arrivals will preserve their mental health and "buy time" to learn more answers, reduce the ambiguity.

Be empathetic. As a way of enhancing your relationships with your hosts, make a conscious effort to be empathetic, i.e., put yourself in the others' shoes. First try to understand, and then try to be understood. Empathy can be practiced by becoming an active listener.

Be flexible and resourceful. To adapt to a new culture, we should understand that flexibility and resourcefulness are key elements. The best-laid plans often are not realized when living and working in a different culture. You need to make and execute new plans quickly and efficiently if plans do not work out as expected and don't become overstressed. Resourceful people are familiar with what is available in the host culture, and know how to take advantage of available opportunities and are comfortable with calling on others for help.

Be humorous. Don't lose your sense of humor. Either at home or abroad, people in any situation tend to get themselves in trouble if they take themselves too seriously. Everyone makes mistakes when struggling to learn a new culture that may be discouraging, embarrassing, or downright laughable. Your hosts will disarmingly forgive your social faux pas in most situations. The ability to laugh at your own mistakes (or at least not lose sight of the humorous side) may be the ultimate defense against embarrassment (蔡绿，2006).

To be certain, no bottled remedies for culture shock are to be found at the pharmacy, but simply know that culture shock exists, that it happens to everyone to some extent, and that it is not permanent and is likely to reduce the severity of the symptoms and speed the recovery. Don't think you are pathological or inadequate if you experience some culture shocks. It is normal that the anxiety resulting from trying to operate in a different environment. Give yourself permission to feel frustration, homesickness, or irritability. Eventually, you will work through these symptoms and come up with a much richer appreciation of the host culture. But it is also important to remain realistic. For purely personal reasons, there may be others who you will not like and vice versa. And there are some things that may never be understood. You can begin to search for solutions once you understand that these problems are perfectly normal reactions for anyone in the same situation.

Key Term

culture shock 文化休克

文化休克由世界著名文化人类学家奥博格（Kalvero Oberg）首先提出。他说："由于失去了自己熟悉的社会交往信号或符号，对于对方的社会符号不熟悉，而在心理上产生的深度焦虑症。"在跨文化管理学中，当人们到国外工作、留学或定居时，常常会体验到不同程度的心理反应，这种心理反应现象被称为"文化休克"。

Glossary

diligent	*adj.* 勤奋的
drag	*v.* 拖；拉；迫使
compliment	*n.* 恭维；称赞
recipe	*n.* 秘诀；药方
alternative	*adj.* 两者择一的；供选择的
downright	*adv.* 彻底地；完全地
severity	*n.* 严重；严肃
knitwear	*n.* 针织品
alleviate	*v.* 减轻；使缓和
mechanism	*n.* 机制
vice	*n.* 缺点；恶习

Comprehension Question

Please list several methods about alleviating culture shock.

Extended Activities

Case Analysis

Case 1

A British young man is talking with his friends about his experience of his first visit to his Chinese tutor, "As soon as I sat down with my tutor, the hostess—my tutor's wife, came up to me with a cup of coffee. I drank ten cups of coffee in less than an hour staying at my tutor's home..."

(Source: 房玉清，姚颖. 跨文化交际实训（第二版）[M]. 北京：对外经济贸易大学出版社，2014.)

Question for Discussion

Is the British student crazy about coffee so that he drinks ten cups of coffee at his tutor's home?

Case 2

Li Hua, a Chinese student studying in Britain, was once invited by her British classmate James to his house to cook a Chinese meal. Her two Chinese friends were also invited. They busied themselves in the kitchen, making dumplings while James did something in the garden and his wife sat on the sofa reading. Li Hua felt a little upset, for she thought that both the host and the hostess should offer to help with the kitchen work. The meal was great and everyone enjoyed themselves. The couple kept complimenting them on their cooking skills and asked for the recipe. But then after the meal, the couple just put down their chopsticks and started minding their own business, leaving the Chinese guests to clear the table and do the dishes. Li Hua felt absolutely confused and even got angry.

(Source: 房玉清，姚颖. 跨文化交际实训（第二版）[M]. 北京：对外经济贸易大学出版社，2014.)

Question for Discussion

How do you understand this case? Should Li Hua get angry?

Case 3

Zhang Yun had just started working for a foreign-owned enterprise. He was sitting at his workstation but had not been given any assignment that he should be doing at this moment. He was relaxing and waiting and then thought he would take the opportunity to have a look around. He poked his head into several offices just to see what there was to be seen.

Suddenly, Mr. White, who also worked in the company, came up to him and angrily asked him what he was doing. Zhang Yun was embarrassed. He laughed and quickly started to move back toward his workstation. This did not seem to satisfy Mr. White who started to talk rapidly and angrily. Hoping to calm him down, Mr. Zhang smiled and apologized, trying to explain that he was trying to learn more about the department. However, Mr. White got even angrier. Finally, another worker came by and calmed him down, but Mr. White left, still looking angry. Mr. Zhang sighed; he knew he had made a bad start but still didn't understand why.

(Source: 房玉清，姚颖. 跨文化交际实训（第二版）[M]. 北京：对外经济贸易大学出版社，2014.)

Questions for Discussion

1. Why did Mr. White get so angry with Mr. Zhang?
2. Can you figure out some differences between Westerners and Chinese from this case?

Case 4

Zhang Zhidong, one of the top officials in the Qing Dynasty, was invited to visit the United States. He was warmly welcomed. One day, Zhang was hosting a banquet for the American officials at a popular restaurant. As the banquet started, according to the Chinese custom, Zhang stood up and said, "I am very happy to have all of you here today. Although these dishes are coarse and not delicious and good enough to show my respect for you, I hope you will enjoy them..."

The next day, the English version of his words was shown in the local newspaper. To his shock, the restaurant owner flew into a rage. He thought it was an insult to his restaurant and insisted that Zhang Zhidong should show him the evidence of which dish damaged the reputation of the restaurant, and he should apologize. All the fuss made Zhang Zhidong rather embarrassed.

(Source: 房玉清，姚颖. 跨文化交际实训（第二版）[M]. 北京：对外经济贸易大学出版社，2014.)

Question for Discussion

Could the Westerners understand Chinese modesty?

Further Reading

Letter to John

Dear John,

A few days ago when I went shopping, I saw a senior Western woman in a store downtown. In Chinese, she was trying to ask a storekeeper if she could buy a certain kind of table. However, she was not good at Chinese, so the storekeeper didn't understand her. She seemed to be getting more and more frustrated, so I went over and asked in English whether she needed help, but she just ignored me and kept trying to explain things to the storekeeper herself. The storekeeper still failed to get her point, so I asked again if I could translate for her. This time she looked at me and said she didn't need my help. She also said that if I wanted to practice English I should go to an English corner. Then she turned around and left the store. She sounded annoyed and looked unhappy, so I didn't follow her to try again.

Why was she so rude and unfriendly? Did I do something improper by asking if I could help her? Don't Westerners ever accept help from other people?

Sincerely,

Li Ling

(Adapted from：斯诺（Don Snow）（美）. 跨文化交际技巧：如何跟西方人打交道（学生用书）修订版 [M]. 上海：上海外语教育出版社，2014.)

John's Response

Dear Li Ling,

Actually I don't know for sure why the lady was so unreceptive toward your offer to help her. Not all Westerners would respond you in such a way—in fact, many would appreciate your offer to help.

From the comment she made to you, it seems that there was some misunderstanding in her that she took your hospitality for a purposeful behavior to practice English—and she wasn't interested in English practice. Indeed, some Westerners in China like to talk with eager Chinese students and don't mind giving them a chance to practice their English, but other Westerners don't like English practice so much. One problem is that Chinese students often practice their English on Westerners more than with them. In other words, they are more interested in practicing English by talking to a real person, and this sometimes makes Westerners feeling used as a tool. Another problem is that English practice is sometimes boring for Westerners: many Chinese students often ask the same questions and talk about the same topic in practicing English with them. Some Westerners may become tired of such affairs.

There may exist another possibility that the woman was trying to practice her Chinese. If that is the case, she may have gotten annoyed because your well-intentioned attempt to help got in the way of her language practice. Unfortunately for foreigners, sometimes there is slim chance in China to practice Chinese because so many Chinese people want to practice English.

It is also probably that she intended to handle the situation herself—even if she wasn't able to do it very well—and didn't want to be interfered with. While Westerners often appreciate the help that Chinese people offer, they sometimes also find Chinese attempts to help a little suffocating because many Westerners like to do things for themselves when possible. It could be that you offered help at a time when the woman was tired of being helped and simply wanted to do things for herself.

Finally, it is also possible that she turned out to be in a bad mood that time. Perhaps you just caught her on a bad day and she took it out on you. Of course this can happen to anyone anywhere, but people who live in foreign countries sometimes become especially tired and irritable because of the strains and difficulties of living in an unfamiliar culture.

That's it. Do not think it too much and just let it go.

Sincerely,

John

(Adapted from：斯诺（Don Snow）（美）. 跨文化交际技巧：如何跟西方人打交道（学生用书）修订版［M］. 上海：上海外语教育出版社，2014.）

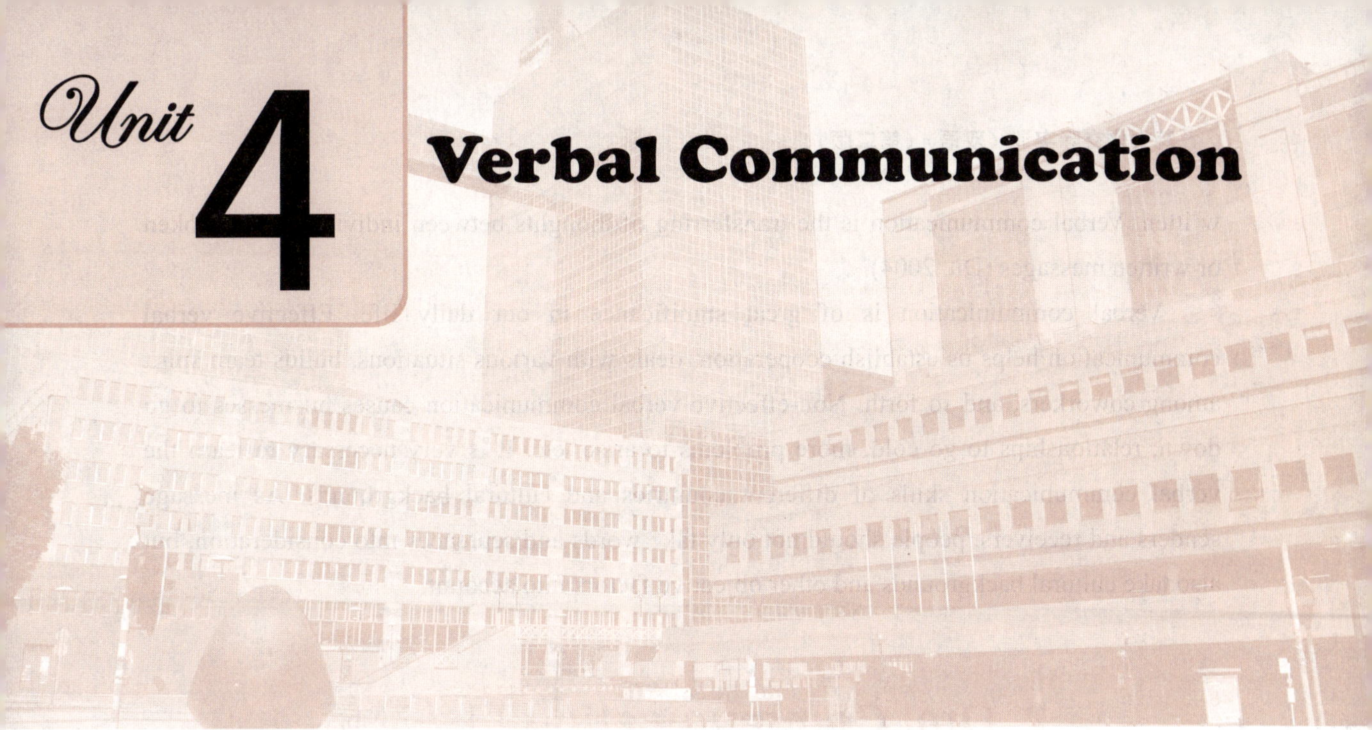

Unit 4 Verbal Communication

Learning Objectives

After learning this unit, you will be able to:

✧ define verbal communication;

✧ describe and classify oral communication and written communication;

✧ understand the accurate usages of both oral and written communication.

Warm-up

1. What are the major differences between Chinese and people from other countries when they talk to each other?
2. Use your own experience or some examples around you to explain the differences.

Focused Study

1. Verbal Communication 言语交际

According to *Longman Dictionary of Contemporary English* (2003), the term "verbal" refers to spoken rather than written. The term "verbal" used here includes both spoken and written. Verbal communication is the transferring of thoughts between individuals via spoken or written messages (Du, 2004).

Verbal communication is of great significance in our daily life. Effective verbal communication helps us establish cooperation, deals with various situations, builds team spirit among coworkers, and so forth. Non-effective verbal communication causes businesses to go down, relationships to go cold, more problems to arise, etc. It is very necessary to learn the verbal communication skills of different countries and cultural backgrounds. As message senders and receivers, people should not only take words and sentences into consideration, but also take cultural backgrounds and other objective factors into account.

2. Oral Communication 口头交际

2.1 Address Form 称呼语

Address form is the correct title or name that people should use when speaking or writing to someone. The choice of address forms is restricted by various factors. In *The Pronouns of Power and Solidarity* (1960), Roger Brown and Albert Gilman held that power and solidarity are the two main factors that restrain people from using address forms. There are many bases of power, which include physical strength, wealth, birth, age, sex, institutionalized role in the state, the army, the church or within the family and so on (Chen, 2002). Solidarity, the general relationship, is symmetrical and reciprocal. It indicates the commonality in some aspects between individuals, such as experience, age, gender, occupation, interest, religion, race, etc.

Assuming that a man named John Miller, who is a senior partner and attorney in a big law firm, let's see how he and other people use address forms in their daily lives.

Scene 1:

(In a café...)

Waiter: Good morning, **sir**. What can I get you?

John Miller: Good morning. I'd like an espresso, please.

Analysis:

"Sir", "Miss/Madam" are much popular in Western countries than in China. Although Chinese people call men "先生" and women "女士", "小姐", they don't want to be too formal and awkward in daily life. People tend to call strangers who are at the same age "大哥" or "大姐" and elder people "大爷" or "大妈". For children and teenagers, they usually call strangers "爷爷" "奶奶" "叔叔" "阿姨", etc. Another common address form "师傅" applies for people of any gender or age and it has the implication of equity. In Western countries, people adopt "Mr.+ Last Name" for all men, "Mrs.+ Married Name (usually husband's last name)" for married women, "Miss+ Last Name" for unmarried women and "Ms.+ Last Name" for women whose marital status are unknown. Different address forms often lead to misunderstandings and embarrassments. When coming to other countries, we intend to be polite and modest by greeting men with "uncle (叔叔)" or "grandpa/grandfather (爷爷)" and women with "aunt (阿姨)" or "grandma/grandmother (奶奶)". We do it by courtesy, but actually it is inappropriate and has exactly the reverse effect. "Uncle" or "aunt" is only used between relatives or used by children, in front of a first name, to address or refer to a man or a woman who is a close friend of their parents. Thus, calling strangers "uncle" or "aunt" will make them feel uncomfortable and confused. "Grandpa/grandfather" or "grandma/grandmother" is only between relatives and therefore calling elder people like this will make them feel incompetent and offended.

Scene 2:

(In court...)

Judge Parker: Counselor, do you have anything to add?

John Miller: Nothing further at this moment, **Your Honor**.

Analysis:

When referring to the address form for man or woman who works at service industries, such as nurse, driver, porter, conductor, counselor, operator, waiter/waitress, steward/stewardess, etc., people usually use job titles instead of names. In some English classes in China, we can sometimes see that conversation:

Teacher: Class begins.

Monitor: Stand up.

Students: Good morning, teacher.

Teacher: Good morning, students. Sit down, please.

In English, both "teacher" and "student" cannot be used as address forms. The precise use of the address forms should be changing "teacher" to "Mr./Ms./Miss+ last name" and "students" to "class".

For people who specialize in some particular kind of work or are in certain position, the address forms can be different. For example, Bishop Gray (格雷主教), Captain Cook (库克船长), Father Brown (布朗神父), General Grant (格兰特将军), Judge Roberts (罗伯茨法官), President Obama (奥巴马总统), Queen Elizabeth (伊丽莎白女王), etc.

In scene 2, the address form "Your Honor" that adopted by John Miller is a polite and dignified way to express people's sincerity and respect. Although it is not a compulsion to use such terms, e.g., "Your Honor" "Your Lordship", etc, while a judge is addressed in a court, the only requirement is to address it in a respectful manner. For other particular figures, we have other forms to address them, such as "Your Majesty" for a king or a queen, "Your Highness" for a member of the royal family, "Your Excellency" for a very important official position, especially an ambassador, "Your Grace" for an archbishop, a duke or a duchess, etc.

Scene 3:

(At his son's college...)

John Miller: Good afternoon, **Prof. Waters**. I'm **John Miller Jr**.'s father. Nice to meet you.

Prof. Waters: Nice to meet you too, Mr. Miller.

Analysis:

"Professor (Prof.)" and "Doctor (Dr.)" are two common address forms. In Germany and other countries, they also have the title "Prof. Dr."

In Western countries, people sometimes give their children the same names as their ancestors'. They adopt generational suffixes to make a distinction between each other. People use "Name+ Sr. (Senior)" and "Name+ Jr. (Junior)", such as Robert John Downey Sr. and Robert John Downey Jr. In order to use suffixes, names (first name, any and all middle names or lack thereof, and last name) must be entirely and exactly the same and this rule has often been abused by many people. Therefore, technically speaking, George Herbert Walker Bush and George Walker Bush cannot be called as "George Bush Sr." and "George Bush Jr." because of the slight difference of their names. Also, "Sr." and "Jr." only apply to living parents and children. For deceased parent or child, their names change to "Name Ⅰ" / "Name, the first" and "Name Ⅱ" / "Name, the second", for example, Johann Baptist Strauss Ⅰ and Johann Baptist Strauss Ⅱ[①]. In China, people avoid using their forefathers' names to call their offspring. They employ "老+last name" and "小+last name" to distinguish between the son and the father. But we cannot simply translate these two Chinese words "老" and "小" into English words "old" and "little".

① For more detailed information, please search: http://schmidtgen.com/wordpress/2013/10/20/how-to-use-jr-sr-ii-iii-etc-with-cartoons.

People are not willing to be called "old" even if they are no longer young. The word "old" is used when people show their sympathy to other people, e.g., "Poor old Tom was sick for weeks." People use "little" in front of others' first names to extend their affection or dislike, e.g., "Look! Little Maya is playing with that dog."

Scene 4:

(At home...)

Mike Miller: Hey, **Johnny**, can you bring me some sugar?

John Miller: Sure.

Analysis:

The official given names of Western people usually contain multiple syllables, such as Abraham. But people prefer to use one or two syllables as their pet names, such as Abe. On ceremonial occasions, people tend to be professional and formal. It is not appropriate to address others by their nicknames unless they give the permission. Also, other intimate address forms, for example, honey, sweetheart, etc. should be used cautiously. Even though people are open-minded these days, we still don't want to touch others' bottom lines. If people are getting along with each other and very close to each other, they can evolve their addresses into more intimate words, such as pet, honey, sweetheart, etc.

2.2 Greetings and Partings 问候语和告别语

Firth (1973) suggests that greetings and partings should not be treated as spontaneous emotional reaction to the coming together or separation of people. For the most part they are

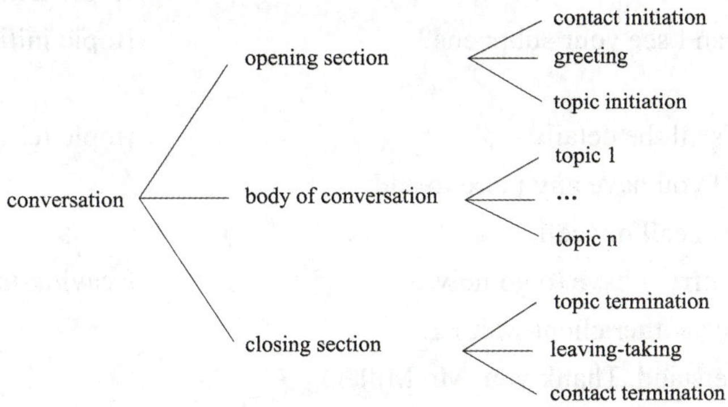

Figure 4-1 Summary Diagram of Clark's Analysis of Conversational Structure

(Source: Qian, 1996)

highly conventionalized and follow patterned routines. Also, greetings and partings are two components of the overall structural organization of conversations (Qian, 1996). According to Clark (1985), a conversation between two (or more) people usually has three major parts: (1) opening section, (2) body of conversation, and (3) closing section. The overall structure and details of each part will be displayed in the following diagram.

In order to clearly show the expression that people use when they are in different occasions, we continue to adopt the examples of John Miller.

Scene 5:

(At the office...)

Client:	Excuse me, madam.	[contact initiation]
Assistant:	Yes? What can I help you, sir?	[topic initiation]
Client:	Is Mr. Miller here? I'm his new client.	[topic]
Assistant:	Yes, please follow me.	
Client:	Thank you.	[topic termination]
...		
John Miller:	Hello, Mr. Fitz. I'm John Miller.	[contact initiation]
Client:	Hello, Mr. Miller.	
	Very nice to meet you.	[greeting]
John Miller:	Me, too. Please take a seat.	
	How are you doing, Mr. Fitz?	
Client:	Not so good.	
	I've got a subpoena from my wife.	[topic initiation 1]
John Miller:	Oh, what happened?	[topic 1]
Client:	I have a drinking problem.	
John Miller:	I see.	[topic termination 1]
	Eh, can I see your subpoena?	[topic initiation 2]
...		
Client:	That's all the details.	[topic termination n]
John Miller:	OK. If you have any more to add,	
	you can call my cell.	
	I am sorry. I have to go now.	[leaving-taking]
	I have another client waiting.	
Client:	I understand. Thank you, Mr. Miller.	
	See you next time.	
John Miller:	See you.	[contact termination]

Analysis:

In the first conversation between the client and the assistant, the greeting and parting are omitted. They are also simplified in conversations between strangers, colleagues, family members, etc. Often, these kinds of dialogues start with some phrases, such as "excuse me" "sorry to interrupt/disturb/bother you", or just with a "hello". The following table will display some examples of greeting and parting from three aspects: time, formality and content.

		Greetings	Partings
Time	All-time (used for any day and at any time)	Hello! Hi! How are you?	Goodbye! See you!
	Real-time (used at a specific time of the day)	Good morning! Good afternoon! Good evening! Good day!	Good day! Good night!
	Seasonal (used only on some special days and other festivals)	Happy New Year! Merry Christmas!	/
	Introductory (used when two people are introduced to each other)	How do you do? I've heard so much about you. I finally have the chance to meet you in person.	/
	Ceremonial (used at birthdays, wedding ceremonies, house-warming parties and other occasions)	Happy birthday! Congratulations!	/
Formality	Formal (used on important occasions where maximum attention needs to be paid to speech and where speakers must be very polite)	How do you do? It is a great honor for me to meet you.	Good day! Have a nice day! Nice meeting you!
	Informal (used in ordinary conversations to create a relaxed language environment)	Hello! Hey! How's everything?	Bye-bye! See you later!
	Familiar (used between intimate friends to enhance solidarity)	How are you getting on? What's up?	So long! Catch you later!
Content	Personal (concerned about the addressee's health, feelings, work and other mentionable personal affairs or belongings)	Direct personal greetings: How are you? How is your family? Are you all right? Indirect personal greetings: This car [i.e. your car] is gorgeous, isn't it?	/
	Non-personal (concerned about weather or other things which are not personal)	Lovely day, isn't it? What weather!	/

Apart from the three aspects that shown in the above table, more classification of greetings and partings should be paid attention to: regionality (British English, American English, Australian English, etc.), settings (service encounter, telephone call, TV/radio broadcast, etc.) and origin (native and foreign).

In China, people usually use some causal topics to open a conversation, for example, "您吃了吗?" "您这是去哪儿啊?" "呦，您在这儿浇花呢？", etc. If we translate these sentences into English, those greetings will make no sense to Western people. When asking "Have you had your dinner?", people may think that you want to ask them out for meals or you want to have a date with them. When asking "Where have you been?" or "Where are you going?", people may feel uncomfortable because you may violate their privacy. When saying "You are watering your flowers, aren't you?", people may think that you are talking trash. Although those greetings are applied well in China, it is awkward and dumb when you use them in Western countries.

Also, there are some conflicts between China and Western countries when people say goodbye to each other. In China, people often say "这么晚了，您该休息了，我就不打扰了" "您这明天上班还得早起呢，我就先告辞了", etc., as their leaving excuses. Also, Chinese people use apologies at parting, for example "不好意思，今天给您添麻烦了". In Western countries, people prefer to find excuses from their own, e.g., "I must go now. My wife is waiting for me at home." "I'm sorry. I've to go. Tomorrow I have an important exam.", etc. Or, people just express their gratitude, such as "I enjoyed the dinner very much. Thank you for your kind hospitality." "I think I'd better go now. Nice talking to you.", etc. At that time, the host would often walk the guest to the front door. In China, the guest may say "请留步" or "不要远送了" and the host may answer "走好" "慢走" "路上注意安全" as partings. If those sentences are literally translated into English, it may cause confusion, for example, "请留步" into "Stay here", "慢走" into "Walk slowly". These expressions may be seen as command to Western people and may make them feel embarrassed. In Western countries, the host may not see you out for a very long distance unless the guest asks for. Often, the guest may say "I'll see myself out" and the host may answer "Do come around again when you have time." or "Give my best regards to your family." as partings.

Scene 6:

(On the phone...)

Assistant: Hello! Spencer & Miller. What can I do for you?

Client: Hello! May I speak to Mr. Miller?

Assistant: Hold on, please. I' ll put you through.

...

Mr. Miller: Hello? Who's speaking?

Client: Hello, Mr. Miller. This is Frank Fitz of Modern Pharmacy returning your call. I'm sorry you missed me when you called my office this morning...

Analysis:

This conversation is very typical in business communication. People often start with greetings, then introduce themselves and ask for the people they want to talk to. For instance, "Hello, this is ××× speaking. Could/May I speak/talk to ××× please?/I'd like to speak/talk to ××× please." If people don't give out their identities at first, the addressee will ask in the following conversation, such as "who's speaking/calling?", etc. In real business telephoning, the situation is more complicated and it is significant for us to be polite and calm.

2.3 Compliments 恭维语

Holmes (1986) believes that a compliment is a speech act which explicitly and implicitly attributes credit to someone other than the speaker, usually the person addressed, for some good (possession, characteristics, skills, etc.) which is positively valued by the speaker and the hearer. Compliment varies from culture to culture and is a highly used polite speech act in people's social communication. Like a mirror, compliment has reflected the most valuable stuff of a particular culture and the culture value of a specific social group. Compliment is frequently applied to create new interpersonal relationship, shorten the social distance, maintain and reinforce solidarity, alleviate contradiction between the speaker and the addressee, etc.

A. Objects

Under the circumstance of Western culture, it is not a big deal for a man to compliment a woman about her appearance, body shape, dressing, etc. Any man can compliment their friend's wife like "Your wife looks gorgeous" or "Your wife is very sexy in that dress". People express their compliment to all ages.

On the contrary, people will feel uncomfortable, if a friend is praising their wife with words with sexual meaning in China. The objects often concentrate on children or senior people.

B. Subjects

In Western culture, people tend to compliment others on the result they gain, not on their prerequisite. For example, "I am so proud of your success." In Chinese culture, people are more likely to praise on personal talent, competence, etc., for example, "你真能干".

Western people compliment others according to the fact and they lay their emphasis on the results. For instance, "You have done a great job." Chinese people incline to regard personal morality and noble mind as their subjects, for instance, "您对学生真负责任".

In Western culture, compliments usually go between people with different social status, especially between superiors and subordinates. People with high social status usually give their credit to people with lower social status in order to maintain a good working relationship. In China, the situation is opposite. Subordinates often compliment their superiors for their abilities and achievements to gain the favor of the "bosses".

In Western culture, when people compliment others, they focus the subject on each other and express their praises in a direct way. In Chinese culture, people sometimes extend their subject to others' family members. It seems that the irrelevant family member gets the complimentary remarks, but the real aim is still to please the addressee. Western people are willing to compliment their family in front of others, such as, "My boy is so sweet." But Chinese people don't like to sing their own praises.

C. Language Forms

(1) Words

According to Manes and Wolfson's research (1981) on American compliments, there are two types of semantic carriers for positively evaluative words: adjectives and verbs. These two kinds of words make up 96% of the total and the use of adjectives are outnumbered the use of verbs. "Nice" "good" "beautiful" "pretty" and "great" constitute two-thirds of the adjectives that employed in compliments. And the two words "like" and "love", which indicates appreciation, occupy 86% of the verbs in compliments.

In Chinese compliments, there are three types of semantic carriers for approved appraisal: adjectives, adverbs and verbs. These three kinds of words account for 90% of the total. The high frequency adjectives are "好" "行", etc., and adverbs are "真" "很" "特". People usually combine those adverbs with adjectives to extend a strong sense of admiration. They seldom adopt the verbs "喜欢" or "喜爱", etc.

Based on the data, researchers compared the words choosing of American and Chinese compliments and found some differences. First, Western people use more adjectives than Chinese people. Second, adverbs are widely used in Chinese compliments and the combination of adverbs and adjectives enhances the power of compliments. Third, American compliments are more formulaic.

(2) Syntax

Manes and Wolfson believe that complimentary remarks have patterns. There are three main forms, which occupy about 85% of the total syntax, in American compliments.

① Noun Phrase+ is/looks+ Adj. (53.6%)

E.g.: Your car is/looks gorgeous.

② I+ (really)+ like/love+ Noun Phrase (16.1%)

E.g.: I really like that painting.

③ Pronoun+ is+ (a)+ Adj.+ Noun Phrase (14.9%)

E.g.: This is a big house.

There are also three main forms in Chinese compliments.

① Noun Phrase+ Adv.+ Adj.

E.g.: 你的车真漂亮。

② Second Person+ V.+ Adv.+ Adj.

E.g.: 你走得真快。

③ Second Person+ Noun Phrase+ V.+ Adj.

E.g.: 你英语说得流利。

We can conclude from the examples that compliments have some patterns to trace and American compliments have more patterns than Chinese compliments. When the subject is pronoun, Western people prefer to use first person, but Chinese people favor second person.

D. Response Patterns

Compliment and response always co-occur. Schegloff and Sacks (1977) think that the compliment event is a two-unit turn adjacency pair. The addressee who receives the compliment should decide whether he/she is going to accept or decline. Due to different values and cultures, Western people are glad to accept compliment with "Thank you" in most cases, but Chinese people are more willing to decline with "哪里哪里" "惭愧惭愧" "过奖过奖", etc. In Western culture, people emphasize individuality and tend to express own views and opinions. In Chinese culture, people deem modesty as virtue. "Complacency spells, while modesty brings benefits." "Modesty helps one go forward, whereas conceit makes one lag behind.", etc., are what people are taught about. Although Chinese people degrade themselves when getting complimentary remarks, it is also noteworthy that people are keeping up with the times, especially the young. People attempt to accept compliments under some situations and feel at ease when they thank others for their compliments.

Herbert's 12 Types of Compliments Responses

1. Appreciation token: a verbal or nonverbal acceptance of the compliment.
   A: You look beautiful today!
   B: Thank you.
2. Comment acceptance: addressee accepts the complimentary force and offers a relevant comment on the appreciated topic.
   A: I love your dress!
   B: Yeah, it's my favorite.
3. Praise upgrade: addressee accepts the compliment and asserts that the compliment force is insufficient.
   A: The dress and those shoes are a perfect match!
   B: Yeah, really brings out the air of lady in me, doesn't it?
4. Comment history: addressee offers a comment on the object complimented, and it shifts the force from the addressee.
   A: The perfume you wear smells sweet!
   B: I bought it for my honeymoon.
5. Reassignment: addressee agrees with the compliment assertion, but shifts the force to some third person or object.
   A: I love your new car!
   B: My parents gave it to me last week.
6. Return: as with reassignment except that the praise is returned to the first speaker.
   A: You haven't changed a bit!
   B: So do you!
7. Scale down: addressee disagrees with the complimentary force, pointing to some flaw in the object or claiming that the praise is overstated.
   A: Look at your bracelet! It's beautiful.
   B: Actually it's quite common.
8. Question: addressee questions the sincerity or the appropriateness of the compliment.
   A: I love your new hairstyle!
   B: Do you really think so?
9. Disagreement: addressee asserts that the object compliment is not worthy of praise; the first speaker's assertion is in error.
   A: Your car is amazing.

B: But I really don't like it.

10. Qualification: weaker than disagreement. Addressee merely qualifies the original assertion, usually with "though" "but" "well", etc.

    A: Your car is amazing.

    B: It's all right, but Miller's better.

11. No acknowledgment: addressee gives no indication of having heard the compliment. He/she either responds with an irrelevant comment (topic shift or gives no response).

    A: Your new boyfriend is handsome.

    B: I think it's going to rain.

12. Request interpretation: addressee, consciously or not, interprets the compliment as a request rather than a simple compliment; it is not actually a compliment response.

    A: This lip gloss is amazing!

    B: You want to borrow this?

2.4 Topic Picking 话题选择

The harmonious interpersonal relationship is hard to maintain. People who are conversation stoppers always bring friendly chats into awkward silences. Wrong topics can be one of the reasons that terminate the conversations. Therefore, choosing proper topics may help maintain good relationship. The following diagram shows the taboo subjects that foreign people are not supposed to raise in conversations.

Topics	Expressions
Age	How old are you? What's your age?
Income	How much do you make/earn? What's your income? How much did it cost you? How much did you pay for that?
Appearance	You've put on weight, haven't you? This color doesn't suit you. You look sick.
Marital Status	Are you married or single?
Politics	Are you a Republican or Democrat? Why did you vote for Donald Tramp?
Religion	Do you go to church? What's your religion?

These topics are just small parts of the taboo topics and everybody has his own topics that they don't want people to raise. It is better for us to talk about common topics until the other person is willing to share part of their privacy with you. Although sometimes people open those taboo topics, we should still be careful about our words when answering. Don't make people feel that you are interfering their businesses.

Key Terms

1. power and solidarity 权势关系与同等关系

1960 年，美国社会心理学家 Brown 和 Gilman 在《表示权势与同等关系的代词》（*The Pronouns of Power and Solidarity*）一文中首次使用“power”和“solidarity”这两个术语，并揭示了称呼的用法既受民族特点、社会结构和集团意识的约束，又与交谈者之间的身份差距及亲疏程度相呼应。人们在社会交往中，人与人之间的关系为不对等的权势关系和对等的同等关系。称谓形式中体现的权势关系（power）和同等关系（solidarity）也是社会语言学研究的重要课题之一。所谓“权势关系”是指“如果一个人在某些方面有某种优势，能控制另一个人的行动，他对后者就具有权势”（郝凤乔，1999）。这是一种非相互的关系，因为两个人不能在某一行动范围内同时对对方拥有权势，因而是一种不对等的关系。而“同等关系”是指双方在交往中因有某种共同点而产生的对等关系，它涉及交往双方共享多少经验，共享多少社会特征，如宗教、性别、年龄、出生地、种族、职业、兴趣等，以及打算在多大程度上共享亲密行为及其他因素（贾玉新，1999）。

2. 外国的“uncle，aunt”和中国的“七大姑八大姨”

中国人重视家庭观念，家庭成员之间的长幼尊序从汉语中大量的表示亲属关系的词语中可以看出来。汉语里对亲属的称谓强调男女有别、长幼有序，如爷爷、奶奶、外公、外婆、姨婆、小舅、小姨、二大爷、三大叔、四大婶、五大嫂、哥哥、弟弟、姐姐、妹妹等。而西方家庭关系相对比较松散，核心家庭只包括父母和子女，成员间的关系比较平等，也不强调父系和母系的区别以及同辈成员间的长幼之分。无论是爸爸还是妈妈的兄弟姐妹，统称“uncle，aunt”，自己的兄弟姐妹不管年长年幼，都只用“brother”或“sister”表示。中国人跟美国人在用汉语交际时，表示亲属关系的词语常常在互相理解对方意思方面会造成很大困难，因为不是所有的称呼都可以找到令人满意的对应词。如果缺乏语境，英语句子“His brother married my sister.”就很难译成汉语（莫爱屏，2016）。感兴趣的同学可以观看美剧《摩登家庭》。通过观看，对比中国家庭成员之间的称呼，可以更加清晰地理解中美之间称谓语的不同。

Glossary

discipline	*n.* 知识领域；（尤指大学的）学科，科目
solidarity	*n.* 同等关系；团结；齐心协力；相互支持
institutionalized	*adj.* 约定俗成的；成惯例的
symmetrical	*adj.* 对称的
reciprocal	*adj.* 互惠的；相应的
commonality	*n.* 共同特征；共性
courtesy	*n.* 礼貌；谦恭；彬彬有礼；（正式场合的）客气话，礼貌话
incompetent	*adj.* 无能力的；不胜任的；不称职的；不合格的
dignified	*adj.* 庄重的；庄严的；有尊严的
compulsion	*n.* 强迫；强制；强烈欲望；（难以克制的）冲动
archbishop	*n.* （天主教、东正教和英国国教的）大主教，主教长
suffix	*n.* 后缀；词尾
syllable	*n.* 音节
conventionalized	*adj.* 成为惯例的；习俗化的
subpoena	*n.* （传唤证人出庭的）传票
real-time	*adj.* 实时的
regionality	*n.* 区域性
gratitude	*n.* 感激之情；感谢
hospitality	*n.* 殷勤好客；热情友爱
confusion	*n.*（尤指因想法不同造成的）困惑，不明确
attribute	*v.* 把……归因于；把……归咎于
alleviate	*v.* 减轻，缓解（痛苦等）
morality	*n.* 道德；道义；伦理
subordinate	*n.* 下级；下属
semantic	*adj.* 语义的
formulaic	*adj.* 程式化的；俗套的；非独创的
syntax	*n.* 句法规则；句法
adjacency	*n.* 邻接；邻近
decline	*v.* 婉拒；谢绝
complacency	*n.* 自满；自得；自鸣得意；沾沾自喜
conceit	*n.* 自负；自高自大；骄傲自大
terminate	*v.* （使）停止，结束，终止

Comprehension Questions

1. Use examples or experience to distinguish the differences between Chinese and Western styles of greetings, partings and styles of compliment.
2. Compare address forms, greetings, partings and different compliments in different occasions.

3. Written Communication 书面交际

3.1 Types of Written Communication 书面交际的类型

Written communication is a communication by means of written symbols. Before the inventions of typewriter and computer, office clerks sat behind the desk laboriously writing stuffs, such as business letters, balance sheets, etc., with pens.

Letter Letter can be long or short. Business letter tends to be short with concise content and precise language. If the business letter is not to the point, people may be distracted by those unnecessary information and forget about the important part that others are trying to get across.

E-mail Electronic mail, as a significant form of written communication, has emerged for decades and it is vital in people's daily communication.

Running record Running record refers to ongoing accounts of work, such as contact records, personal visits, office appointments, letters and phone calls.

Referral Referral is a request for an assessment or a service. It includes the basic information needed to begin to form a picture of the situation and it also needs to be clear what is being requested and why.

Report Written report is an official document which people issue after investigating a situation or event. The basic principle of report writing is the need to match the report to the specific requirement and ensure that the report is appropriate to its purpose.

Assessment Assessment is a consideration of someone or something and a judgment about them or a calculation or estimate of the value of something.

Summary Summary is an important part in maintaining the thread of ongoing work by drawing together key themes and issues. Also, it is used when work comes to an end.

Agreement Written agreement can be known as contract. It is very critical when one company is developing partnership or achieving change with another one. Accurate and appropriate use of terms and words are required in written agreements. Vagueness in the way the agreement is phrased can lead to great difficulties later in the process.

Message Apart from the texts that people send to each other, leaving telephone message is another way to contact and communicate. Some telephones have the auto answering machines and people can directly leave a message. But in some companies, telephones are often picked up by assistants, at this time clear and precise message is very significant.

3.2 Key Issues 注意事项

Purpose There are three questions people need to ask themselves when undertaking written communication: (1) who will be reading the written work; (2) what it will be used for; and (3) what the writer hopes it will achieve.

Relevance A major issue here is the content: what people shall include and what people shall leave out. Either too much information or too little information may cause troubles. Too much "padding" is both a waste of time and effort on the part of the writer and a distraction on the part of the reader. Information omitted or glossed over may also be less than satisfactory. People should find the balance between these two extremes by providing the minimum of information necessary, not the maximum available.

Planning If people start to write without considering some key points, then the likelihood of a successful outcome will be seriously undermined. The key points include: (1) what points are to be made; (2) what order they should be in; and (3) what level of formality is appropriate.

Clarity Effective written communication depends to a large extent on clarity: (1) avoid long, cumbersome sentences that are confusing and difficult to follow; (2) avoid ambiguity and vagueness and beware of words or phrases that can be misinterpreted or that are imprecise to be of value; (3) present work appropriately; and (4) do not rely on jargon or technical terms that others may not be able to understand.

3.3 Basic E-mail Structure 电子邮件的基本格式

Nowadays, although sometimes people still write things to each other, they prefer to use e-mails to deliver their messages. E-mails shorten the time people communicate with each other. However, writing business e-mails in English is not an easy thing to do. People can explain and redress ourselves due to others' facial expressions and reactions when having face-to-face communications. However, in e-mails, inappropriate use of words, phrases and sentences and subtle differences in tone may lead to big misunderstandings.

Subject 主题
Salutations 称呼语 Introduction 导语/开头 Body 正文 ● 好消息 (Good news) ● 坏消息 (Bad news) ● 请求 (Request) ● 道歉 (Apologies) ● 意见和建议 (Opinion) ● 可选项：告诉对方有附件 (Attachments) Closing 结束语

Subject:

E-mail has become part of this "information sea". Everyday people are bombarded with endless e-mails, such as personal e-mails, business e-mails, commercial e-mails, junk mails, etc. With so many e-mails in one inbox, people tend to read the subject first, then to decide whether they open the e-mail or not. In this case, a clear and conspicuous subject may attract people's attention. The subject of the e-mail should be as specific as the newspaper's title. Too short subject (1-2 words) may cause misunderstanding, but too long (over 10 words) may also lead to verbosity.

Good example:

□ My ideas for ××× project

□ Friday staff meeting minutes

□ X8 model development update

Salutation:

1. "Dear + Mr./Ms./Prof./Dr. + last name" + ","

   E.g.: Dear Mr. Miller,

   Dear Ms. Collins,

2. "Dear + job title/company name" + ","

   E.g.: Dear Purchasing Manager,

   Dear Customer Service,

   Dear Kevin & Associates,

3. "To Whom It May Concern (相关人士)"
4. "Hi/Hello" + first name (for intimates)

Introduction:

In introduction, people often say something to express their gratitude, apology, reason to write, etc.

For example:

Thank you for.../This is in regards to.../I'm writing to...

Closing:

Whether good news or bad news, gratitude, apology or favor in the e-mails, people usually give positive response to look forward to future cooperation, even if the cooperation may become a long shot.

For example:

We look forward to hearing from you.

If you have any questions, please feel free/don't hesitate to contact me.

I hope that we have adequately addressed your concerns.

Complimentary Closing:

Three types of complimentary closing indicate the degree of relationship from informal to formal (left to right).

Regards, Best regards, Best wishes, As ever, Thanks!	Sincerely, Sincerely yours, Yours sincerely, Cordially, With best regards, Warmest regards,	Yours truly, Very truly yours, Respectfully, Respectfully yours,

Key Term

business e-mail 商务电子邮件

成功的商务电子邮件的特点：(1) 正文简洁明了：一封邮件应该只为一个目的而写，越简洁越有诚意，要开门见山，避免使用长句及套语；(2) 使用简单、口语化的表达用语：用口语化的句子写电子邮件，多使用 "you" "I" 和 "we"，避免使用过时的表达用语及过多行话，在很多情况下简单的单词表达的意思更明确；（3）使用郑重的表达用语：对简单的邮件进行简单的回复，慎重选择表达语气，电子邮件没有表情、手势、音调；（4）避免使用命令语气："must"和"have to"都带有命令的语气，多用"please"和"could you"，要强调对方的利益；（5）使用主动语态：原则上多用主动语态，除传达不好的消息或想被认定为受害者时；（6）多用并列结构；（7）收集整理电子邮件常用语；（8）通过语篇标记词衔接前后内容；（9）更多考虑收件人的情况：考虑对方的身份，是否为专业领域的专家等（Kevin Kyung, 2013）。

Glossary

laboriously	*adv.* 耗时费力地；辛苦地；艰难地
referral	*n.* 移交；送交
gloss over	掩饰；掩盖；把……搪塞过去
undermine	*v.* 破坏，损害（某人的努力或成功的机会）
cumbersome	*adj.* 冗长的；累赘的；复杂的
jargon	*n.* 行话；行业术语

Comprehension Questions

1. Use examples or experience to distinguish the differences between Chinese and Western e-mail writing habits.
2. Try to write a business e-mail and summarize some common conjunctions and usage of words when writing e-mails.

Extended Activities

Case Analysis

Case 1

Vijay is a student from India who has just arrived in the United States to attend graduate school at a major university. Vijay began to learn English in primary school, and since his field of study is engineering, even his classes in the program leading to his bachelor's degree were conducted in English. Vijay considers himself to be proficient in the English language. Nevertheless, during his first week on campus, the language of those around him is bewildering. People seem to talk so fast that Vijay has difficulty differentiating one word from another. Even when he recognizes the words, he can not quite understand what people mean by them. His dormitory roommate seemed to say, "I'll catch you later" when he left the room. The secretary in the departmental office tried to explain to him about his teaching assistantship and the students assigned to the classes he was helping to instruct. Her references to students who would attempt to "crash" the course were very puzzling to him. His new faculty advisor, sensing Vijay's anxiety about all of these new situations, told him to "hang loose" and "go with the flow". When Vijay inquired of another teaching assistant about the meaning of these words, the teaching assistant's only reaction was to shake his head and say, "Your advisors from another time zone!" Needless to say, Vijay's bewilderment continued.

(Source: Lustig M, Koester J. Intercultural Competence: Interpersonal Communication Across Cultures (7th ed.) [M]. New Jersey: Pearson Education, Inc., 2013.)

Questions for Discussion

1. What happened to Vijay?
2. Why is this kind of phenomenon occurred around the oversea students?

Case 2

Airport ride request:

(1)

American 1: We're going to New York this weekend.

American 2: What fun! I wish we were going with you. How long are you going to be there? *(If she wants a ride, she will ask.)*

American 1: Four days. By the way, we may need a ride to the airport. Do you think you can take us?

American 2: Sure. What time?

American 1: 9 a.m. this coming Saturday.

(2)

Chinese 1: We're going to New York this weekend.

Chinese 2: What fun! I wish we were going with you. How long are you going to be there?

Chinese 1: Four days. *(I hope she'll offer me a ride to the airport.)*

Chinese 2: *(She may want me to give her a ride.)* Do you need a ride to the airport? I'll take you.

Chinese 1: Are you sure it's not too much trouble?

Chinese 2: It's no trouble at all.

(3)

Chinese: We're going to New York this weekend.

American: What fun! I wish we were going with you. How long are you going to be there?

Chinese: Four days. *(I hope she'll offer me a ride to the airport.)*

American: *(If she wants a ride, she'll ask me.)* Have a great time.

Chinese: *(If she had wanted to give me a ride, she would have offered it. I'd better ask somebody else.)* Thanks. I'll see you when I get back.

(Adapted from: Ting-Toomey S. Communication Across Cultures [M]. Shanghai: Shanghai Foreign Language Education Press, 2007.)

Questions for Discussion

1. Distinguish the differences among the three scenes.
2. Explain the reasons.

Further Reading

English Names

Names are a cultural universal. This means everyone uses names. A person's name can tell us a bit about a person's family. We'll begin by looking at first names and how English people choose names for their children.

Let's take a brief look at first, or given names. There are several ways parents choose the first name for their child.

The first way is by family history. Parents may choose a name because it is passed from generation to generation; for example, the first born son might be named after his father or grandfather. Although family names are also passed to daughters, it is usually used as a middle name. Adding "junior" or "the second" is only done with boys', not with girls'.

The second way parents choose a name is after a family member or friend who has died recently, or after someone they admire, like a well-known leader or famous musician.

The third way is to provide a "push" for the child. Parents want to choose a name that sounds very "successful". A strong name might help them in the business world, for example.

Let's look at the origin of the last names, also called family names or surnames. Researchers have studied thousands of last names, and they've divided them into four categories. The categories are: place names, patronymics, added names, and occupational names.

The first category is place names. Place names usually identified where a person lived or worked. Someone named John Hill live near a hill, for example, and the River family lived near a river.

The second category is patronymics. A patronymic is the father's name, plus an ending like sen or son. The ending means that a child, a boy is the son of his father. Robertson is the son of Robert, for example.

The third category is added names. Linguists sometimes call this category "nickname", and the word "nickname" is actually an old English word that means an additional name, an added name. This category of last names is fun because the names usually described a person. Reed was from "red" for the red hair. Baldwin was someone who was bald, with little or no hair.

The fourth category is occupational names. The origin of the family name was the person's occupation. The most common examples of occupational names still used today are Baker (someone who bakes bread), Tailor (someone who sews clothes), Miller (someone who makes flour for bread) and Smith. Smith is actually the most common name in the Western English-speaking world. The name comes from an Old English word smite, which means to hit or strike. In the old days, a smith made metal things for daily life, like tools. Every town needed smiths. What interesting is that many languages have a family name that means Smith.

Though names may tell us someone's family history, they may not tell us much at all about the present. For example, there's usually not much connection between the origin of the name and the person who has it now. Take the name Cook, for instance. A person named Cook today probably doesn't cook for a living.

Names are different all over the world. In some countries, family name comes before the given name. In the Muslim world, a girl's name includes her father and grandfathers' names. In China and Japan, there is no middle name. I think it's interesting how people choose a name. In many countries, each name has a special meaning.

Unit 5 Nonverbal Communication

Learning Objectives

After learning this unit, you will be able to:

✧ define nonverbal communication;

✧ identify nonverbal behavior and know the meaning behind;

✧ understand how nonverbal communication influences our daily lives in every aspect.

Warm-up

1. Does sign language belong to nonverbal communication?
2. Use your own experience or some examples around you to explain the importance of nonverbal communication.

Focused Study

1. Nonverbal Communication 非言语交际

1.1 Definition of Nonverbal Communication 非言语交际的定义

Although spoken language can be deployed to solve some problems of social complexity, nonverbal communication is the speediest, most effortless and historically developed means for adapting to the social world.

To most people, nonverbal communication refers to communication effected by means other than words, assuming words are the verbal element. Like most definitions, this one is generally useful, but it does not account for the complexity of this phenomenon adequately. Sign language is movements of hands and arms used to communicate by deaf people. These gesticulations are mostly linguistic (verbal), yet hand gestures are often considered behavior that is "other than words". McNeill (1992) demonstrated the linguistic qualities of some gestures by noting that different kinds of gestures disappear with different kinds of aphasia—the impairment of the ability to use or comprehend words—namely, those gestures with linguistic functions similar to the specific verbal loss. Conversely, not all spoken words are clearly or singularly verbal, for example, onomatopoeic words (buzz, murmur, etc.) and non-propositional speech used by auctioneers and some people with aphasia.

The definition reads as "Nonverbal communication involves all those nonverbal stimuli in a communication setting that are generated by both the source and his or her use of the environment and that have potential message value for the source or receiver." (Samovar et al., 2000) This definition includes the automaticity and control in nonverbal behavior. As with mist social activity, the production of nonverbal behavior is neither fully automatic nor fully controlled. Unlike most social activity, however, some nonverbal behaviors are nearly impossible to consciously start or stop and nonverbal behavior is often initiated and executed without intention. Moreover, people are surprisingly unaware of the form that their nonverbal behavior takes. Although some nonverbal behaviors can be controlled, particularly in the service of impression management and meeting social norms (DePaulo, 1992), the control of nonverbal behavior appears to be taxing and reduces capacities for the performance of other tasks (Richeson & Shelton, 2003). For every nonverbal behavior we control there is another that cannot be simultaneously controlled, suggesting that at any point in (social) time people exhibit spontaneous nonverbal behavior.

1.2 Functions of Nonverbal Communication 非言语交际的功能

Ekman (1965) identified six important ways of verbal and nonverbal behaviors interrelate during human interaction.

Repeating Nonverbal communication can simply repeat or echo what was said verbally. This has the effect of clarifying or reinforcing the verbal messages. For example, people may tell others to go north to find a parking place and then point in the proper direction.

Conflicting Verbal and nonverbal signals can be at variance with one another in a variety of ways. They may communicate two contradictory messages or two messages that seem incongruous with each other. For example, the public speaker, who, with trembling hands and knees and beads of perspiration on the brow, claims, "I'm not nervous." In some cases it is a natural response to a situation in which communicators perceive themselves to be in a bind. They do not want to tell the truth, and they do not want to lie. As a result, their ambivalence and frustration produce a discrepant message (Bavelas et al., 1990). In other situations, conflicting messages occur because people do an imperfect job of lying. Displays of incongruous or conflicting signals may occur in a variety of ways.

Sometimes two nonverbal signals may manifest the discord (e.g., vocal with visual), but usually we are more aware of the contrasting verbal and nonverbal signals (e.g., positive voice/negative words, negative voice/positive words, positive face/negative words, or negative face/positive words). Leathers (1979) has identified a common three-step process for people to react when confronted with conflicting messages that matter to us: (1) the first reaction is confusion and uncertainty; (2) search for additional information that will clarify the situation; and (3) if clarification is not forthcoming, people will probably react with displeasure, hostility, or even withdrawal.

Whether people rely more on what a person says or does nonverbally may depend on what they are trying to figure out about that person. Hall and Schmid Mast (2007) showed that people turn relatively more to nonverbal cues when they want to know how a person is feeling and more to verbal cues when they want to know what a person is thinking.

Complementing Nonverbal behavior can modify or elaborate on verbal messages. When the verbal and nonverbal channels are complementary, rather than conflicting, our messages are usually decoded more accurately. Some evidence suggests that complementary nonverbal signals also may be helpful when attempting to recall the verbal message. For example, when the senior manager praises his employee, the action of patting on the shoulder of the fellow by the manager at the same time will put extra meaning to such a message.

Substituting Nonverbal behavior can also substitute for verbal messages. It may indicate more permanent characteristics (sex, age), moderately long-lasting features (personality, attitudes, social group) and relatively short-term states of a person. For example, a nod of the head may be used to indicate "yes", without the word "yes" actually being spoken. Sometimes, when substitute nonverbal behavior does not get the desired response, the communicator tries to verbally clarify the message. For example, a woman who wants her date to stop trying to become physically intimate with her by stiffening, staring straight ahead, or acting unresponsive. If the suitor still does not stop, she might say something like "Look, Bill, please don't ruin a nice friendship."

Accenting/Moderating Nonverbal behavior may accent (amplify) or moderate (tone down) parts of the verbal message. For example, a parent may forbid a child from doing a particular thing by saying the word "no" and reinforcing this by shaking the head and wagging the index finger from side to side.

Regulating Nonverbal behavior is also used to regulate verbal behavior: (1) by coordinating our own verbal and nonverbal behavior in the production of our messages; and (2) by coordinating our verbal and nonverbal message behavior with those of our interaction partners. For example, posture changes may demarcate a topic change; a gesture may forecast the verbalization of a particular idea; pause may help organize spoken information into units.

Key Term

functions of nonverbal communication 非言语交际的功能

（1）一般功能：言语交际是线性的，它的信息传播是单通道的，而非言语交际信号是全方位的立体传输。非言语交际既可以补偿言语信号暂时性的停顿和间隙，又能够帮助人们表达内心深处思想、意愿的交际方式和意图。非言语交际的自身特点主要表现在两个方面：a. 信息容量具有不确定性。信息容量的大小，在很大程度上依赖对方的感受。b. 含义的模糊性和随意性。非言语交际不像言语表意那样比较明了固定，但作为非言语信息的接受者却能把这种模糊变得相对清晰。就言语交际而言，非言语行为对话语意思的表达具有重复、否定、补充、替代、强调和调节等辅助作用。

（2）社会功能：英国非言语行为学者 M. Argyle 在《人类社会互动的非语言沟通》中曾指出：非语言行为沟通的社会功能涉及三方面：a. 处理、操纵直接的社会情境；b. 辅助语言沟通；c. 代替语言沟通（莫爱屏，2016）。

Glossary

complexity	*n.* 复杂性；错综复杂
gesticulation	*n.* 手势；示意动作
impairment	*n.* 损害；损伤；障碍
onomatopoeic	*adj.* 拟声的；象声的
auctioneer	*n.* 拍卖人；拍卖商
aphasia	*n.* 失语症
stimuli	*n.* 促进因素；激励因素；刺激物
bead	*n.*（液体的）小滴
perspiration	*n.* 汗；汗珠
ambivalence	*n.* 矛盾情绪；矛盾心理；摇摆；犹豫
discrepant	*adj.* 差异的
discord	*n.* 不一致；不和；纷争
forthcoming	*adj.* 即将来临的；即将发生的
hostility	*n.* 敌意；对抗；敌对行为
withdrawal	*n.* 撤走；收回；取回
complementary	*adj.* 互补的；补充的；相互不足的
stiffen	*v.*（肌肉或关节）变得僵硬；（使）变得不灵活
wag	*v.*（通常指由于厌恶而）左右摇晃（手指）
demarcate	*v.* 划定……的界线（或界限）

Comprehension Questions

1. Which is more important, verbal communication or nonverbal communication? Explain why.
2. Role play: use nonverbal expressions only and perform a real-life situation.

2. Body Language 体态语

Body language, also known as body movements, body behavior etc., includes all expressions and movements which send communicative messages. Birdwhistell called the study of body language or how movement communicates "kinesics". In general, kinesics cues are those visible body shifts and movements that can send message about our attitude toward the other person, our emotional state and our desire to control our environment (Samovar et al., 2000). Facial expression, gesture, posture, eye contact and touch will be touched upon respectively.

2.1 Facial Expression 面部表情

Your face, my thane, is a book where men may read strange matters.

—Shakespeare, Macbeth, Act Ⅰ

The face is rich in communicative potential. It is a primary site for communication of emotional states, it reflects interpersonal attitudes, it provides nonverbal feedback on the comments of others, and some scholars say it is the primary source of communicative information next to human speech (Knapp et al., 2014). Because of these reasons and the visibility of faces, people rely heavily on facial cues when making significant interpersonal judgment. As infants, babies take special interest in facial expressions that their parents and relatives display and they even mimic them.

Although facial expressions are visible, people are no dumb. Sometimes, people try to hide their feeling by neutralizing their facial expressions. When people wear a "mask", it is hard for others to read the poker face. Still, there will be traces of evidence to tell people's emotion.

Many factors influence how emotions are inferred from the face, but the compelling fact remains that they can be inferred and often with extremely high levels of accuracy. Some emotions are more likely to be confused, but six basic emotions showed below are judged with very high accuracy among observers in many studies.

The six basic emotions with a description of their characteristic facial actions are from the studies of Ph.D. Paul Ekman and other scholars.①

Surprise The brows are raised so they are curved and high. The skin below the brow is stretched, and horizontal wrinkles go across the forehead. The eyelids are opened: the upper lid is raised, and the lower lid is drawn down; the white of the eye—the sclera—shows above the iris and often below as well. The jaw drops open so the lips and teeth are parted, but there is no tension or stretching of the mouth.

Fear The brows are raised and drawn together. The wrinkles in the forehead are in the center, not across the entire forehead. The upper eyelid is raised, exposing the sclera, and the lower eyelid is tensed and drawn up. The mouth is open and the lips are either tensed slightly and drawn back or stretched and drawn back.

Disgust The upper lip is raised. The lower lip is also raised and pushed up to the upper lip, or is lowered and slightly protruding. The nose is wrinkled and the cheeks are raised. Lines show below the lower lid and the lid is pushed up but not tense. The brow is lowered, lowering the upper lid.

Anger The brows are lowered and drawn together and vertical lines appear between them. The lower lids are tensed and may or may not be raised. The upper lids are tensed and may or may not be lowered by the action of the brow. The eyes have a hard stare and may have a bulging appearance. The lips are in either of two basic positions: pressed firmly together, with the corners straight or down, or open and tensed on a squarish shape, as if shouting. The nostrils may be dilated, but this is not essential to the anger facial expression and may also occur in sadness. There is ambiguity unless anger is registered in all three facial areas.

Happiness The corners of the lips are drawn back and up. The mouth may or may not be parted, with teeth exposed or not. A wrinkle, the nasolabial fold, runs down from the nose to the outer edge beyond the lip corners. The cheeks are raised. The lower eyelids show wrinkles below them and may be raised but not tense. Crow's-feet wrinkles go outward from the outer corners of the eyes.

Sadness The inner corners of the eyebrows are drawn up. The skin below the eyebrows is triangulated with the inner corner up. The upper eyelid inner corners are raised. The corners of the lips are down, or the lips are trembling.

Although the six basic emotions of facial expression can be judged with high accuracy, Russell (1994) found that facial expression, mainly of Westerners' faces, were more accurately

① If you are interested, you can read the book entitled *Nonverbal Communication in Human Interaction (8th edition)*, chapter 9, page 279-281.

recognized by other Western groups than by non-Western groups. An in-group advantage had been documented, showing that people in the same cultural, national or ethnic group have an advantage when judging cues expressed by their members.

2.2 Gesture and Posture 手势及姿势

We respond to gestures with an extreme alertness and, one might say, in accordance with an elaborate and secret code that is written nowhere, known by none, and understood by all.

—Edward Sapir

Gestures perform many intrapersonal and interpersonal functions. Typically, gestures are thought of as arm and hand movements, but head gestures are also well known.

"OK" sign With index finger and thumb held in a circle and the other three fingers extended, palm outward, people can easily pose an "OK" sign. In America and Britain, it means "OK" and "great". In France, it means "zero" or "worthless". In Thailand, it means "no problem". In Japan, Myanmar and Republic of Korea, it means "money". In India, it means "yes". In Tunisia, it means "fool". In Greece, it has the offensive meaning. In a few countries, it apparently denotes a particular body orifice. In China, this sign can be recognized as "three", "zero", "no problem" and "OK".

"Thumb-up" sign In North America, it means "hitchhike". In Sri Lanka, Mexico and the Netherlands, it means "pray for luck or blessing". In Japan and Republic of Korea, it means "man" "your father" and "old man". In Greece, it means "enough". In Nigeria and Australia, it means "rude". In China, America and Britain, this sign contains the meaning of "great" "incredible" "praise", etc.

"V-shaped" sign With index finger and middle finger extended into a V-shaped and curved thumb pressured on the ring finger and little finger, this V-shaped sign may cause some problem when people use it. This sign was first invented by Victor de Laveleye and promoted by Winston Churchill. If the "V-shaped" sign is flashed with palm outward, it means "victory" and general approval. But if the sign is posed with palm facing yourself, it apparently means something close to "up yours" or "screw you".

"Finger-crossing" sign With index finger and middle finger crossed and curved thumb pressured on the ring finger and little finger, this "finger-crossing" sign may lead to some misunderstanding. In America, France, the Philippines, Malaysia and Mexico, it means "pray for luck or blessing". In Australia, it means "expectation". In India, it means "finished or done". In Sri Lanka, it means "evil". In the Netherlands, it means "swear" or "oath". In some European countries, it means "insult" or "hostility". In China, it means "number ten" "plus" or "good luck".

Other "famous" gestures Charles de Gaulle, former president of France, was noted for his grasping gesture which many felt signified his desire to control the subject under discussion. Angela Merkel, German Chancellor, was noted for her symmetric gesture "Merkel's Rhombus" or "Triangle of Power", which stands for both power and stability.

Posture People sometimes use some body movements to express their emotions. With two arms up in the air gives people an impression of arrogance. Crossing arms is a protective posture and may suggest threat to others. Shrugging shoulders can express one's indifference, innocence or powerlessness. Hands on the waist indicates direct intrusion into others' affairs and this posture is regarded as aggressive and not considerate enough.

For example, the poster of Jackie Chan's 2002 movie *The Tuxedo* encountered many problems in Thailand. The locals were much offended by Jackie Chan's posture in this poster because they think feet are inferior and dirty.

Identifying Difference: Posture and Sitting Habits

Posture and sitting habits offer insight into a culture's deep structure. In many Asian cultures, the bow is much more than a greeting. It signifies the culture's concern with status and rank. In Japan, for example, low posture is an indicator of respect. Although it appears simple to the outsider, the bowing ritual is actually rather complicated. The person who occupies the lower station begins the bow, and his or her bow must be deeper than the other person's. The superior, on the other hand, determines when the bowing is to end. When the participants are of equal rank, they begin the bow in the same manner and end at the same time.

The manner in which we sit also can communicate a message. In the United States, where "casualness" is considered a great virtue, people often sit with feet on chairs or even desks. They sometimes sit with their backsides (buttocks) on tables and desks as a way of expressing their individuality or carefree attitude. Slumping oneself over while sitting in a chair and placing feet on whatever object around is a common American behavior. It is intended to show that the person is casual, honest, sincere and "just one of the folks".

Unfortunately, people of other countries may interpret this behavior as being sloppy and as reflecting a general lack of alertness, interest and respect. Americans do not usually realize that what they think of as casualness is viewed very differently and very negatively by many people around the world. People in many cultures are expected to sit erect. Such cultures include many countries in Latin America, Asia, Europe and the Middle East.

In America, crossing legs is a sign of good etiquette. Americans feel comfortable crossing their legs and sitting with one ankle on the other knee. Many cultures say that crossing legs is okay, but placing the ankle on the knee while crossing one's legs is totally unacceptable. You can cross your legs but not put your ankle on your knee in some Latin and Asian countries. In Peru, men can place the ankle on knee, but women must cross their entire legs at the knee. In Syria women must not cross their legs at all in public, though men can cross at the knee.

One reason for not putting the ankle on the knee is that when you do so, one foot or the sole of the shoe is usually pointing at someone. This is a very severe insult in many countries around the world, especially Muslim countries.

(Source: Xu Lisheng. Intercultural Communication in English (Revised Edition) [M]. Shanghai: Shanghai Foreign Language Education Press, 2015.)

2.3 Touch 触感

We often talk about the way we talk, and we frequently try to see the way we see, but for some reason we have rarely touched on the way we touch.

—Desmond Morris

Touch serves many functions and conveys many messages and the act of touching is like any other message we communicate: It may elicit positive, neutral or negative reactions, depending on the configuration of the touch, the people involved and the circumstance. Morris (1977) reported on field observation that led to the naming of 457 types of body contact, falling into 14 major types of public body contact occurring between two people. Major categories of nonaggressive touching include the following:

Handshake The strength of the tie or desired tie between the participants can often be observed by watching the shaking hand. We can always see people shaking hands to show their politeness, especially on political occasions.

Body-guide Touching is a substitute for pointing here. The person guiding the other's body is frequently the person in charge during that encounter.

Pat When adults pat other adults, it is often a condescending gesture or congratulatory pat. For example, a supervisor may pat the shoulder of his employee when he wants to encourage him.

Arm-link This may be used for support when one person is infirm, but it is also frequently used to indicate a close relationship.

Shoulder embrace This half-embrace is used in male-female romantic relationships as well as to signify buddies in male-male relationships.

Full embrace or hug This gesture frequently occurs during moments of intense emotion, sporting events, romance, greetings and farewells. It is also used ritualistically to show a relationship closer than a handshake would indicate.

Hand-in-hand When adults hold hands with children, it is designed for support, to keep children close, or to protect them. As adults, handholding suggests an equality within the relationship, because both parties are performing the same act. It is often thought of in opposite-sex relationships, but same-sex handholding is not uncommon, even between males (e.g., children, high-contact cultures).

Waist embrace According to Morris, the waist embrace is frequently substituted for the full embrace when the participants wish to signal more intimacy than handholding or a shoulder embrace yet still remains mobile.

Kiss The location, pressure, duration and openness of a kiss help signal the closeness or desired closeness between two people at a particular moment.

Hand-to-head Given the highly vulnerable nature of the head area, letting someone touch us on the head shows a trusting, often intimate, relationship.

Head-to-head Two people touching heads render them incapable of regarding other ongoing activities in a normal manner, so this is usually thought of as an agreement by both parties to shut out the rest of the world—a condition especially common to young lovers.

Caress This signal is associated with romantic feelings for a partner, although like any signal, it can be used by non-intimates who are trying to deceive others about the depth of their relationship.

Body support Parents often support children by carrying, lifting or letting them sitting in their laps. Such support may be sought among adults in playful situation, or when one person feels physically helpless.

Mock attack Aggressive-looking behaviors are sometimes performed in a nonaggressive manner: for example, arm-punches, hair-rufflings, pushes, pinches and ear-nibbles.

In business, we can only see few postures, such as handshake, pat and so forth. People may avoid much touch when they first meet each other. In some cultures, shaking hands is the only form of public touch. For example, in England, shaking hands lightly is fine, but other forms of touching (such as backslapping or putting an arm around the shoulder of a new acquaintance) are not common. People from such diverse cultures as the South Pacific, Eastern and Western Europe, and even the Far East and parts of Africa greet each other with a handshake and may wave at each other at a distance. In most of these countries other forms of touching in public are generally not encouraged. In some other countries (in parts of Europe, Latin America and the Middle East), handshaking can be followed (or substituted for) by an embrace or a kiss on the cheek.

Matching Task

When trying to communicate cross-culturally, we frequently face a myriad of potential communication hazards. Not only do different cultures speak unintelligible languages, but their body languages are often mutually incomprehensible as well. Different gestures may serve the same function, and the same gesture can have a number of unanticipated consequences when dealing with people from different cultures. Think over how to convey the following meanings with different gestures in different cultures? How to beckon somebody to come over in America, the Middle East, Portugal, and Tonga respectively? How to point something or somebody out in America, Mongolia, India, and Guinea-Bissau respectively? How to show approval in France, Greece, Tonga, and Kenya respectively? What is the appropriate type of handshake in America, France, Japan, and the Middle East respectively? What may the folded arms suggest in America, Russia, Finland, and Wales respectively? What may the tug on one's earlobe suggest in Greece, Spain, Portugal, and Scotland respectively? What may the OK sign mean in Brazil, Russia, France, and Japan respectively?

(Adapted from: Xu Lisheng. Intercultural Communication in English (Revised Edition) [M]. Shanghai: Shanghai Foreign Language Education Press, 2015.)

2.4 Eye Contact 眼神交流

He speaketh not; and yet there lies a conversation in his eyes.

—Henry Wadsworth Longfellow

It is common to associate various eye movements with a wide range of human emotions or traits: downward glances are associated with modesty; wide eyes with frankness, wonder, naivete or terror; generally immobile facial muscles and a rather constant stare with coldness. Also, society has established a number of eye-related norms: It is impolite to look too long at strangers in a public place; we are not supposed to look at various parts of the body except under certain conditions, to name a few.

Kendon (1967) identified four functions of gazing: (1) regulatory—responses may be demanded or suppressed by looking; (2) monitoring—people may look at their partner to indicate the conclusions of thought units and to check their partner's attentiveness and reactions; (3) cognitive—people tend to look away when having difficulty processing information or deciding what to say; and (4) expressive—the degree and nature of involvement or emotional arousal may be revealed through looking.

For a good intercultural communication, people should make proper eye contact, even when they are not talking with each other. But in some Asian countries, it is better for men not to stare at or look at women straightly and too long while talking and listening. Sometimes, women tend to use closed posture and other body languages to avoid the straight sight from a man. In Mexican culture, when spoken to by an adult, children show their respect by bowing heads instead of looking the adult directly in the eye.

When a person looks sideways, it shows coldness and arrogance to his or her audience. Moving head side to side is not a polite manner while communicating with others. People who are talking with you may think that you are not attentive and showing no interest in the talk.

Key Term

facial expressions 面部表情

东西方的面部表情存在较大的差异性。西方人面部表情丰富，亚洲人则喜怒少形于色。微笑的次数、产生微笑的刺激物以及微笑传递的社交意义都因文化而异。美国人的微笑表示快乐、友好、高兴、情绪高昂，他们笑是因为他们认为某件事很滑稽；日本人的微笑有同样的含义，然而当问及他们的看法时，却笑而不答，日本妇女常常会因为慌乱或尴尬而微笑；在韩国，笑得太多被认为是肤浅的表现；泰国人却不以为然，他们笑口常开，故泰国有“微笑的国度”的美誉。英语国家的人们认为，过于含蓄的中国人，他们的喜怒哀乐常常不形于色，即使家庭遭遇不幸也要笑脸迎人，这是很多外国人无法理解的事情（莫爱屏，2016）。

Glossary

kinesics	*n.* 身势学
compelling	*adj.* 令人信服的；有说服力的；引人入胜的
index finger	食指
lid	*n.* 眼睑；眼皮
sclera	*n.* 巩膜
protrude	*v.* 突出；伸出；鼓出
bulge	*v.* 凸出
nostril	*n.* 鼻孔
dilated	*adj.*（使）（血管）扩张；（使）（瞳孔）放大
nasolabial	*adj.* 鼻唇的
intrusion	*n.* 侵扰性的事情；扰乱；侵犯

ritualistically	*adv.* 仪式地
hair-ruffling	拨乱头发
ear-nibble	轻咬耳朵
backslap	*v.* 拍背以示友好

Comprehension Questions

1. How do we Chinese people use eye contact in communication?
2. Use examples or experience to distinguish the meanings of different gestures and postures in different countries.

3. Paralanguage 副语言

I understand a fury in your words
But not the words.

—*Shakespeare, Othello, Act IV*

3.1 Voice Quality and Vocalization 音色及发音

The physical mechanism for producing nonverbal vocal qualities and sounds, also called paralanguage, are extremely complex (Juslin & Scherer, 2005). In general, paralanguage has two components: voice quality and vocalization. Voice quality contains pitch, range, resonance, lip control and articulation control. Vocalization involves three parts: (1) vocal qualifiers (volume, pitch, rhythm, tempo, resonance, tone); (2) vocal characterizers (laughing, crying, yelling, moaning, whining, belching, yawning); (3) vocal segregates ("un-huh" "shh" "uh" "mmmh" "humm"). Vocal cues indicate people's personalities, emotional states, socioeconomic status, sex, height, weight and age identification (Su, 2006).

Try to use different voice quality and vocalization to read the sentences below. You can add some vocal characterizers or vocal segregates in the sentences.

(1) **He** borrowed 1,000 dollars from me.

(2) He **borrowed** 1,000 dollars from me.

(3) He borrowed **1,000 dollars** from me.

(4) He borrowed 1,000 dollars from **me**.

In addition to its role in personality and emotional judgments, the voice also plays a part in retention and attitude change, which has been primarily studied in public speaking. Typical prescriptions for use of the voice in delivering a public speech include the following:

1. Use variety in volume, rate, pitch and articulation. The probability of desirable outcomes is less when we use a constant rate, volume, pitch and articulation. Being consistently over-precise may be as ineffective as being overly sloppy in articulation.

2. Base decisions concerning loud-soft, fast-slow, precise-sloppy, or high-low on what is appropriate for a given audience in a given situation.

3. Avoid excessive non-fluencies (Knapp, Hall & Horgan, 2014).

3.2 Silence 沉默

Silence serves as a very significant form of paralanguage, such as soundless reaction or pause. Silence can often say as much as words and it indeed be a powerful message. Cross-cultural differences are common over when to talk and when to remain silent, or what a particular instance of silence means. In response to the question, "Will you marry me?" silence in England would be interpreted as uncertainty. In Japan it would be interpreted as acceptance. In Ibo, it would be considered a denial if the woman were to continue to stand there, and an acceptance if she ran away (Xiong, Liu et al., 2010, p322).

Silent cues affect interpersonal communication by providing an interval in an ongoing interaction during which the participants have time to think, check or suppress an emotion, encode a lengthy response, or inaugurate another line of thought. Silence also helps provide feedback, informing both sender and receiver about the clarity of an idea or its significance in the overall interpersonal exchange (Samovar et al., 2000).

Chinese and American cultures vary from each other and they emphasize speaking and silence differently. According to Edward T. Hall who categorized cultures as being either high or low context, Chinese culture belongs to the group of high-context cultures. Meaning, therefore, is not necessarily contained in words. Information is provided through gestures, the use of space and even silence. However, American culture is part of low-context cultures, which indicates that the verbal message contains most of the information and very little is embedded in the context or the participants. In China, there's a famous saying: "Silence is golden." Silence is a sign of politeness and contemplation and Chinese people tend to be quiet when listening to the lecture or report and they seldom ask any question or answer the question that the speaker asks. By contrast, American audience are likely to be active than the Chinese. They think that silence communicates awkwardness and causes people to be uncomfortable.

Key Term

paralanguage 副语言

副语言指人们在日常言语交际中的说话方式，包括说话人说话时所使用的频率、声调、音高、重音等。频率有快慢之分；声调可分为升调和降调；声音的高低可以决定它是否悦耳，其抑扬顿挫能够左右观众的注意力；音量可以影响信息所传递的含义；一个词的词重音在句中会因与其他词语的组合而消失或得以加强。

Glossary

resonance	*n.* 共鸣；共振
articulation	*n.* 说话；吐字；发音
tempo	*n.*（乐曲的）速度；拍子；节奏
moan	*v.* 呻吟；抱怨
whine	*v.* 抱怨；唠叨
belch	*v.* 打嗝
yawn	*v.* 打哈欠
retention	*n.* 保留；保持
inaugurate	*v.* 为……举行落成仪式；为……举行成立典礼

Comprehension Question

Use different voice quality and vocalization to express a sentence.

4. Object Language 客体语

By a man's finger-nails, by his coat-sleeve, by his boots, by his trouser-knees, by the callosities of his forefinger and thumb, by his expression, by his shirt-cuffs—by each of these things a man's calling is plainly revealed. That all united should fail to enlighten the competent inquirer in any case is almost unconceivable.

—*Sherlock Holmes*

Body smell It is obvious that vision and hearing are the most important sensors for social situations in Western societies, but the sense of smell also may influence responses. The scientific study of the human olfactory system is in its infancy, but we each have an "olfactory signature". Our reactions may be consciously or unconsciously processed, but the message can be quite strong. During heightened emotional arousal, chemical olfactory signals may even assume an importance that rivals the normally dominant visual and auditory channels. Several experiments attest to the fact that people are usually able to identify the odors of specific other human beings. Smells not only help us identify people, but may also play a role in relationship development and maintenance. When unmarried women were asked to select a male's T-shirt that had an odor that they would like to smell if they had to smell it all the time, they selected T-shirts from males who were genetically similar, but not too similar, to their fathers (Jacob, McClintock et al., 2002). The role of odors in human interaction varies considerably from culture to culture. Asians are reported to manifest underarm odor only rarely, but odor seems to play a prominent role in some Arab countries.

Olfactory occupies a prominent place in Arab life. Not only is it one of the distance-setting mechanisms, but it is a vital part of a complex system of behavior. Arabs consistently breathe on people when they talk. However, this habit is more than a matter of different manners. To the Arab good smells are pleasing and a way of being involved with each other. To smell one's friend is not only nice but desirable, for to deny him your breath is to act ashamed. Americans, on the other hand, trained as they are not to breathe in people's faces, automatically communicate shame in trying to be polite (Hall, 1966).

In addition to human odors, environmental odors also may affect human encounters by setting the mood or bringing back memories associated with the smell.

Clothes To understand the relationship between clothes and communication, we must be familiar with the various functions clothes can fulfill: decoration, physical and psychological protection, sexual attraction, self-assertion, self-denial, concealment, group identification, persuasion, attitude, ideology, mood reflection or creation, authority, and status or role display (Barnard, 2001). For example, women's dissatisfaction with their body was related to the greater use of clothing for camouflage purposes. Clothing was a means of communicating messages about the wearer, and liking for a particular outfit was "related to the extent to which this message is similar to the subject's ideal self-image" (Gibbins, 1969). A new outfit may promote feelings of gaiety and happiness; people may feel less efficient in shoes that hurt, and self-consciousness may result from wearing an "inappropriate" outfit, a common feeling for adolescents trying to grapple with their own self-image. Some graduate teaching assistants wear suits to class to distinguish themselves from their students who frequently are almost the same age.

Artifacts and decorations should be taken into consideration when we talk about clothing because they are also potential communicative stimuli. People adorn themselves with badges, tattoos, masks, earrings, personal aid and devices (glasses, watches), accessories (hats), and jewelry, among other things. We know people sometimes react strongly to a particular artifact or decoration. These reactions may be positive, negative or a mixture of the two depending on your point of view. For example, lipstick may be used to enhance the redness of females' lips due to its positive association with greater femininity and attractiveness (Stephen & McKeegan, 2010). Due to concerns that jurors would not give a man accused of murder a fair trial, his lawyer convinced the court to have his client's offensive tattoos cosmetically covered up during trial, suggesting that automatically negative associations of guilt and criminality are linked to the presence of specific tattoos.

Others There are other factors that influence the interpersonal communication, such as attractiveness and the face, body shape, height, body image, body color, body hair (hair-style), etc.

Key Term

cultural differences in clothes 服饰习惯的文化差异

服饰习惯是非言语交际的重要组成部分，可以反映各国文化的特色。某些颜色包含着法律或道德的约束力，具有普遍的意义。如交通指示灯中的红色和绿色及战争时期投降时使用的白旗。由于民族文化、历史和习俗的差异，不同颜色具有不同的象征意义。中国新娘穿红色，因为中国文化把红色看成幸福与吉祥的象征。西方新娘穿白色，因为白色被视为贞操与纯洁的象征。中国殡葬披麻戴孝，用白色表明悲痛；西方人葬礼穿黑色衣服，以黑色寄托哀思。

Glossary

olfactory	*adj.* 嗅觉的
arousal	*n.* 唤起；激起
camouflage	*n.* 伪装；掩饰
grapple	*v.* 努力设法解决
artifact	*n.* 人工制品；手工艺品
femininity	*n.* 女性气质
criminality	*n.* 有罪；犯罪行为

Comprehension Questions

1. Find more objective factors that affect interpersonal communication.
2. Find some dressing taboos in different countries and explain the reasons.

5. Environmental Language 环境语

5.1 Time 时间

Ordinary people merely think how they shall spend their time; a man of talent tries to use it.

—Arthur Schopenhauer

Time language, which refers to how we give meaning to time and how it is communicated to others, is a powerful element of nonverbal communication (Lesikar & Flatley, 2004:427).

There are three types of time system: technical, formal and informal. Technical time is often used by scientists and technicians. Formal time is known by everyone and well worked into daily life. Informal time, such as "a while" "later" "in a minute", etc., is situational and imprecise. Distinctions between different time cultures are mainly manifested on informal time. Michael Argyle compares cultural differences in punctuality standards:

"How late is late? This varies greatly. On the one hand, in Britain and America one may be 5 minutes late for a business appointment, but not 15 and certainly not 30 minutes late, which is perfectly normal in Arab countries. On the other hand, in Britain it is correct to be 5 to 15 minutes late for an invitation of dinner. An Italian might arrive 2 hours later, an Ethiopian after and a Japanese not at all—he had accepted only to prevent his host from losing face."

Edward T. Hall (1959) proposed that cultures organize time in one of two ways: either monochronic time (M-time) or polychronic time (P-time). M-time people think of time in linear terms and schedule one activity at a time, emphasizing schedules, segmentation and promptness, such as people from Germany, Austria, Switzerland, America, etc. P-time people are more flexible and humanistic in time arrangement and emphasize people more than schedules, such as people from Arabs, native Hawaiians, Africans, Spanish, Greeks, Chinese, Mexicans, etc. M-time people tend to think time as something fixed in nature, but P-time people tend to believe time is less tangible. M-time people feel much more guilty if they waste their time than P-time people.

Table 5-1　　Comparison of M-Time and P-Time People

Monochronic-Time People	Polychronic-Time People
Do one thing at a time	Do many things at once
Concentrate on the job	Easily distracted and subject to interruptions
Take time commitments (deadlines, schedules) seriously	Consider time commitments an objective to be achieved, if possible
Low-context and need information	High-context and already have information
Committed to the job	Committed to people and human relationships
Adhere to plans	Change plans often and easily
Concerned about not disturbing others; follow rules of privacy	More concerned with people close to them (family, friends, and close business associates) than with privacy
Show great respect for private property; seldom borrow or lend	Borrow and lend things often and easily
Emphasize promptness	Base promptness on the relationship
Accustomed to short-term relationships	Have strong tendency to build lifetime relationships

(Source: Edward T Hall, Mildred Reed Hall, Yarmouth. Understanding Cultural Differences: Germans, French and Americans[M]. ME: Intercultural Press, 1990.)

5.2　Space 空间

Spatial changes give a tone to a communication, accent it, and at times even override the spoken word.

—E. T. Hall

Signs reading "Keep Out" "Private Property" "Staff Only" are attempts to regulate space among human beings. People do not put up signs in daily conversation, but they use other signals to keep some distance from other people, avoid uncomfortable crowding and other perceived invasions of personal space.

Anthropologist Edward T. Hall identified four types of informal space: (1) intimate, (2) casual-personal, (3) social-consultative, and (4) public. According to Hall, intimate distances range from actual physical contact to about 18 inches (about 45.72 centimeters); casual-personal extends from 1.5 to 4 feet (about 121.92 centimeters); social-consultative, for impersonal business, ranges from 4 to 12 feet (about 365.76 centimeters); and public distance covers the area from 12 feet to the limits of visibility or hearing. These distances are based on

Hall's observation of a particular sample of adults from business and professional occupations, primarily white middle-class native to the northeastern United States.

These distances are not always fixed. People change their position and distance during the course of conversation. There are other variables that may affect the distance relationship.

Table 5-2 Different Dimensions of Personal Space between China and America

Personal Space	Chinese Dimension	American Dimension	Related Circumstance	Related Persons
Intimate distance	0-30 cm	0-45 cm	for most private relations and activities	within couples, with one's parents or children
Personal distance	30-70 cm	45-120 cm	person-to-person intercourse	between friends, acquaintances and relatives
Social distance	70-250 cm	120-360 cm	formal conversation, doing business or social gatherings	colleagues, business associates, between salespersons and customers, unfamiliar faces, etc.
Public distance	more than 250 cm	more than 360 cm	speeches in public and presentations to groups	between speakers and audiences, teachers and students, etc.

(Source: Xiong Lijun, Liu Xuedong, et al. Foundations of Intercultural Communication[M]. Shanghai: Shanghai Jiaotong University Press, 2000.)

Topic or subject matter Leipold's (1963) work demonstrates how anticipated treatment of the same general topic can influence conversational distance. Students entered a room and were given either a negative comment ("Your grade is poor, and you have not done your best"); praise ("You are doing very well, and Mr. Leipold wants to talk to you further"); or a neutral comment ("Mr. Leipold is interested in your feelings about the introductory course"). Students given the negative comment sat farthest from the experiment; those who were praised sat closest. Following insults, people may want to assume a greater distance than they normally would with that person, particularly if the person giving the insult is perceived as a higher-status person (O'Neal et al., 1980). Regardless of topic, very close distances may result in generally less talking (Schulz & Barefoot, 1974).

Setting for the interaction Obviously, the social setting makes a great deal of difference in how far we stand from others in conversation. A crowded cocktail party demands a different distance than a comfortable evening in the living room with a spouse or significant other. Lighting, temperature, noise and available space affect interaction distance. Some authors have hypothesized that as room size increases, people tend to sit closer together. Noisy urban street locations outside an office building may prompt people to stand closer to one another than they do when conversing inside the building. And if the setting is perceived as formal or unfamiliar, we would predict greater distance from unknown others and closer distances to known others.

Physical characteristics Height seems to make a difference in the distance people select for interacting. Irrespective of sex, shorter individuals seem to invite smaller interpersonal distances than taller individuals (Caplan & Goldman, 1981). When the two communicators are vastly different in height, the distance has to be adjusted so faces can be seen. Evidence also indicates that obese people are accorded greater interaction distances (Lerner et al., 1975). Studies by Kleck (1969) point out that when people with physical disabilities expect others to behave in a distant manner.

Attitudinal and emotional orientation Some experiments have been conducted by telling a person that he or she was going to interact with a person who was either "warm and friendly" or "unfriendly". Not surprisingly, greater distances were chosen when interacting with a person perceived to be unfriendly. Similarly, when told to enter into conversation with another person and to behave in a friendly way, people chose closer distances than when told to "let him/her know you aren't friendly". This friendly/unfriendly relationship to distance seems to manifest itself even with preschool children (King, 1966). In some instances, our anger will cause us to withdraw from others, but if we seek retaliation, we may increase proximity (Meisels & Dosey, 1971). Variations in our emotional states, such as depression, fatigue, excitement, or joy, can sometimes make vast differences in how close or far away we want to be from others. A study reported by Patterson (1968) indicates that we may make a variety of interpersonal judgments about others based on distance. Barring any contradictory information, people choosing closer distances are often seen as warmer, more likable, more empathic and more understanding. When we seek to win another's approval, we reduce conversational distance as opposed to instances when we are deliberately trying to avoid approval. Females seeking approval maintained a mean distance of 57 inches; those trying to avoid approval averaged 94 inches. When the distance was held constant at 5 feet, approval seekers compensated by smiling more and engaging in more gestural activity (Rosenfeld, 1965, 1966).

Characteristics of the interpersonal relationship A number of studies also show that conversational distance varies as a function of our relationship with the other person. Strangers begin conversations at a greater distance than acquaintances, and acquaintances are a bit more distant than friends. Preschoolers seem to be able to use distance as a criterion for determining liking or disliking. Like adults, children seem to maintain greater distances with unknown adults, unfriendly or threatening persons, teachers and endomorphs (i.e., those with a heavyset body type). These and other studies suggest that closer relationship is likely to be associated with closer interaction distances. Obviously, there is a point at which we would not expect interactants to get any closer, no matter how their relationship. And even people who are very close will not always interact at close distances due to the ebb and flow of their relationship.

Personality characteristics The bulk of evidence seems to indicate that introverts tend to stand farther away than extroverts and to generally prefer greater interpersonal distances. Other studies suggest that anxiety-prone individuals maintain greater distances, but closer distances are seen when people have a high self-concept and affiliative needs or when they are low on authoritarianism, high on interdependence and "self-directed". People with various personality abnormalities can probably be counted on to show greater non-normative spatial behavior, choosing interactive distances both too far away and too close.

Key Terms

1. time 时间

在一元时间文化的人看来，来自多元时间文化的人们时间观念不强，他们办事较为拖沓。而多元时间文化的人却认为，他们能在同一时间内处理不同的事务，这样会更有弹性，更具人性化。拉丁美洲国家、南欧、非洲、阿拉伯地区和某些亚洲国家属于多元时间文化。

2. space 空间

人类学家根据身体距离的理论，将社交文化分为两种：体触文化与非体触文化。体触文化指身体的接触，是借身体间的接触来传达或交流信息的交际行为，是一种重要的非语言交际方式。体触行为进入了最敏感的近体交际的亲密距离，最易产生敏感的反应。一些国家的人频繁使用体触，其形式多样，并富有强烈的感情色彩，体现极强的文化特色。相反，非体触文化中鲜有身体接触。因此，在跨文化交际中需要谨慎对待，认真了解每一种体触行为的含义及其文化差异。

Glossary

monochronic	*adj.* 出现一次的
polychromic	*adj.* 多次发生的
segmentation	*n.* 分割；切分
humanistic	*adj.* 人本主义的；人文主义的
predominantly	*adv.* 最显著地；占主导地位地

alienate	*v.* 使疏远；使不友好
intermediate	*adj.* 中等程度的；中级的
anticipate	*v.* 预期；预料；预计
hypothesize	*v.* 假设；假定
empathic	*adj.* 感情移入的
endomorph	*n.* 内胚层体型（偏向于圆形）
introvert	*n.* 内向的人；不喜欢与人交往的人
affiliative	*adj.* 有亲和力的

Comprehension Questions

1. Use examples or experience to explain the space you keep in your daily life.
2. What do you think of the time concept of polychronic-time people?

Extended Activities

Case Analysis

Case

During Bill Clinton's presidency, he travelled to China and, at one stop during the trip, spoke to university students in Beijing. President Clinton's remarks were generally well received and were followed by a lively question and answer session. When interviewed for the American press, one student remarked, "During the question and answer period, I did not understand why the president pointed his finger at us to select a person. We would not use such a rude gesture." Puzzled, the American reporter asked the student what gesture the president should have used. The student answered using a sweep of the open hand-palm upward.

(Source: Lustig M, Koester J. Intercultural Competence: Interpersonal Communication Across Cultures (7th ed.) [M]. New Jersey: Pearson Education, Inc., 2013.)

Questions for Discussion

1. What triggered this student's utterance?
2. What should we do when we encounter a different culture?

Further Reading

Top 10 Nonverbal Communication Tips

Kendra Van Wagner

Good communication skills can be very helpful in your lives, and research has shown that nonverbal behaviors make up a large percentage of our daily interpersonal communication. How can you improve your nonverbal communication skills? Paying attention to the following points can help you learn to read the nonverbal signals of other people and enhance your own ability to communicate effectively.

Nonverbal Signals

People can communicate information in such numerous ways as eye contact, gesture, posture, body movements and tone of voice. All of these signals can convey important information that isn't put into words. By paying closer attention to other people's unspoken behaviors, you will improve your own ability to communicate nonverbally.

Incongruent Behaviors

Careful attention should be paid to those whose words do not match their nonverbal behaviors. For example, someone might tell you they are happy while frowning and staring at the ground. Research has shown that when words fail to match up with nonverbal signals, people tend to ignore what has been said and focus instead on unspoken expressions of moods, thoughts and emotions.

Tone of Voice

Tone of voice can be very informative, suggesting enthusiasm, disinterest or anger. Start noticing how your tone of voice affects how others respond to you and try using tone of voice to emphasize ideas that you want to communicate. For example, if you want to show genuine interest in something, you can use an animated tone of voice.

Eye Contact

Failing to look others in the eye can always be interpreted as evading or trying to hide something. But too much eye contact can seem confrontational or intimidating. While eye contact is an important part of communication, it's important to remember that good eye contact does not mean staring fixedly into someone's eyes. Some communication experts recommend intervals of eye contact lasting four to five seconds.

Signals as a Group

A single gesture can mean something, some things, or maybe even nothing at all. The key to accurately reading nonverbal behavior is to look for groups of signals that reinforce a common point. If you place too much emphasis on just one signal out of many, you might come to an inaccurate conclusion about what a person is trying to communicate.

Context

Word has no meaning till it is in a context. When communicating with others, you always keep in mind the situation and the context in which the communication occurs. Some situations require more formal behaviors that might be interpreted very differently in any other setting. Consider whether or not nonverbal behaviors are appropriate for the context, and try to make your signals match the level of formality necessitated by the situation.

Signals to Be Misread

The case that a firm handshake indicates a strong personality while a weak handshake is taken as a lack of fortitude illustrates an important point about the possibility of misreading nonverbal signals. A limp handshake might actually indicate something else entirely, such as arthritis. Always remember to look for groups of behavior. A person's overall demeanor is far more telling than a single gesture viewed in isolation.

(Adapted from: *Bridge Between Minds: Intercultural Communication*. 重庆：重庆大学出版社，2011.)

Unit 6 Business Customs and Etiquette

Learning Objectives

After learning this unit, you will be able to:

✧ know about cultural differences in greeting, making introduction, dining practices, gift giving, tripping and business card exchange;

✧ understand how position and status affect cultural interaction;

✧ understand the importance of knowledge of male and female relationship to successful intercultural communication.

Warm-up

1. How are business customs and etiquette across cultures different from domestic ones?
2. Use examples to explain the cultural differences in business customs and etiquette.

Focused Study

1. Greeting 打招呼

Greeting is the first opportunity to make a good impression in the business world. While due to cultural variations and differences, forms of greeting may vary greatly from the East to the West.

1.1 Verbal Greeting 言语问候

Verbal greeting is customary globally although distinct variations may occur from culture to culture. For instance, Americans may just say “Hi!” or “Hello!” to strangers, which seems quite informal to people from other countries. However, this informality of the American way of greeting is just their unique expression of outward friendliness. Whereas in China, people tend to greet others saying “Where are you going?” or “Have you eaten?” This may seem a little private to the Western people but actually this is Chinese way of showing friendliness.

In order to convey more sincere greetings to people from different parts of the world, the proper choice of greetings may include “Hello, it’s pleased to meet you”, or “Good morning, how are you?”, etc. Appropriate greetings are always safe and keep you away from mistakes in business mingling.

1.2 Non-verbal Greetings 非言语问候

The most common forms of non-verbal greetings include handshake, bowing, hugging and kissing.

Handshake is customary in many countries of the world. Many countries like China, India, Egypt, Finland, Britain, Germany, US, Nigeria, Kenya, etc., all consider handshake as a norm in interpersonal communications. What is noteworthy is that even handshakes may vary accordingly in different countries and cultures.

Table 6-1 Handshakes by Culture

Culture	Type of Handshake
American	Firm
Asian	Gentle (shaking hands is unfamiliar and uncomfortable for some; the exception is the Korean, who usually have a firm handshake)
British	Soft
French	Light and quick (not offered to superiors); repeated on arrival and departure
German	Brusque and firm; repeated on arrival and departure
Latin American	Moderate grasp; repeated frequently
Middle Eastern	Gentle; repeated frequently

(Adapted from these books: *International Business Etiquette: Asia and the Pacific Rim (2002); International Business Etiquette: Europe (1999); International Business Etiquette: Latin America (2000)* by Ann Marie Sabath, Franklin Lakes, NJ: Career Press.)

Bowing is a typical form of greeting in Japan. Bowing in Japan is considered as a way to show respect and is seldom done in Europe.

Although a kiss or hug is considered a little inappropriate as a form of greeting in some Asian, Northern European and North American countries as people in those countries are uncomfortable with touching and hugging; it is a very customary way of greeting in many other countries, for example, in Saudi Arabia, the handshake is accompanied with a light kiss; even males in Saudi Arabia kiss both cheeks after a handshake. In Russia, the "bear hug" may follow a strong, firm handshake between good male friends; people in Latin American countries also embrace, often accompanied by a couple of slaps on the back (Samovar, Porter & McDaniel, 2009).

Key Terms

1. business etiquette 商务礼仪

商务礼仪可以定义为在商业活动中应该遵守的行为规范。

2. way of greeting 打招呼的方式

不同国家有不同的风俗，见面礼仪和打招呼的方式也不同。随着对外交往越来越多，人们跟外国人打招呼的频率也在增加。无论采取什么形式，都要按照他们本国的称呼习惯，这样才比较妥当。

3. kissing 亲吻

在意大利、西班牙和欧洲大部分国家，两个人打招呼的方式都是走上前快速地亲吻彼此的脸颊：先是右侧，然后左侧。如果彼此不太了解，也可以通过握手以示友好。这种打招呼的方式在大多数欧洲国家是一种惯例。

4. bowing 鞠躬

日本是一个极其注重礼节的国家，见面时一般都要互相问候，脱帽鞠躬，眼睛向下，表示诚恳的态度。

Glossary

brusque	*adj.* 唐突的；直率的；无礼的
customary	*adj.* 习惯的；通常的
departure	*n.* 离开；出发；违背
etiquette	*n.* 礼节；礼仪；规矩
friendliness	*n.* 友谊；亲切；亲密

informality	*n.* 非正式；不拘礼节
mingling	*n.* 混合；交际；联合（mingle 的 ing 形式）
outward	*adj.* 向外的；外面的
Saudi Arabia	*n.* 沙特阿拉伯
slap	*vt.* 拍击

Comprehension Questions

1. What are business customs and etiquette?
2. How do handshakes vary accordingly in different countries and cultures?

2. Superstitions and Taboos
迷信和禁忌

Superstitions are beliefs that are inconsistent with the known laws of science or what a society considers to be true and rational. For example, some special charms, omens, or rituals are believed to have supernatural powers. In different parts of the world, people hold different superstitions and it is wise and appropriate to treat certain beliefs seriously with respect when doing business with certain people.

2.1 Superstitions 迷信

As is known to all, 13 is an unlucky number in America due to the Christian religion history. While in China, number 4 is considered to be unlucky due to its similar pronunciation with the Chinese word "death". In some cultures, people also hold other superstitions. For example, sweeping the floor on New Year's Day may sweep away your good luck for the coming year; likewise, bathing on this day washes away your good luck. Giving too much attention to a newborn places the child in jeopardy; the evil spirits will harm the baby if it receives a lot of attention (Dresser, 2005). In many South American countries, people respect some other superstitions like scheduling important events on Tuesday the 13th should be avoided as this is an unlucky day (Bosrock, 1997b).

2.2 Taboos 禁忌

Taboos are practices or verbal expressions considered by a society or culture as improper or unacceptable. Taboos are often rooted in some moral judgment and religious beliefs and handed down from one generation to another. In international business negotiations, taboo-breaking can result in certain degree of embarrassment and hard feelings and it is highly recommended to avoid taboo-breaking by learning taboos in different cultures and countries before one begins to involve in international business.

In Islamic countries, smoking is strictly prohibited during Ramadan. Even foreigners cannot smoke in front of the local Muslims, for it would cause great resentment. Besides, in Arab countries, it is considered taboo to ask about the health of a man's wife. In Asian countries, messages or names should not be written in red ink in many places such as in Republic of Korea, etc., for it has negative associations or even death connotations (Lewis, 2006). In some parts of Asia, fortune-telling and palmistry can be significant means by which business decisions are made, and it is best to respect these beliefs when doing business with people who take business advice from seers. In Japan, people have a strong aversion to things decorated with the images of fox and badger, as these two kinds of animals are considered as representation of greed and deceit.

People from different countries also have different preferences for colors. For example, in Japan, people usually avoid black and dark grey. Italians consider purple as negative. In Brazil, purple and yellow together may bring bad omen, and brown is seen as unlucky. Thai people prefer bright color, and black is for funerals. In India, black, white and light colors are considered unpopular. Mexican people do not like purple and black.

Key Term

superstition 迷信

不同国家迷信的内容或许不同，但几乎所有国家都存在迷信。

Glossary

aversion	*n.*	厌恶；讨厌的人
badger	*n.*	獾；獾皮
	vt.	纠缠不休；吵着要；烦扰

connotation	*n.* 内涵；含蓄；暗示；隐含意义
deceit	*n.* 欺骗；谎言；欺诈手段
funeral	*n.* 葬礼；麻烦事
	adj. 丧葬的；出殡的
greed	*n.* 贪婪；贪心
jeopardy	*n.* 危险；（被告处于被判罪或受处罚的）危险境地
omen	*n.* 预兆；征兆
palmistry	*n.* 手相术
prohibit	*vt.* 阻止；禁止
Ramadan	*n.* 斋月（伊斯兰教历的九月，等于 Ramazan）
rational	*adj.* 合理的；理性的
resentment	*n.* 愤恨；怨恨
ritual	*n.* 仪式；惯例；礼制
supernatural	*adj.* 超自然的；神奇的；不可思议的
superstition	*n.* 迷信
taboo	*n.* 禁忌；禁止

Comprehension Question

What are superstitions and taboos in business world?

3. Holidays and Holy Days 节假日

Holidays and holy days obviously play an important role in people's life in any single country throughout the world. And to businesspeople who conduct business with overseas countries, it is highly recommended to learn about other culture's holidays and holy days, because during these days celebration is on and business may not be conducted at all. Respecting the customs associated with these special days can be a polite and appropriate behavior. Some major holidays and holy days in several major countries will be briefly mentioned as follows.

In America, the most important days are Christmas, Thanksgiving, Eastern, Independence Day, etc. Business is rarely conducted during these days as people may be busy gathering together with their friends and family, or go out celebrating with fireworks, picnics, parades and parties. Some business may even be closed on Sunday due to religious observances, for

Sunday is Sabbath for Christians. Therefore, it is better to schedule your business trips or telephones some other time rather than during these holiday seasons.

In some European countries like France, August is considered a vacation month, and many people might go out on vacation, therefore their businesses are also closed. So it is better not to expect to conduct business in these countries during this month. In some Catholic countries, there is a carnival season, and it is also recommended not to have business plans during this time.

The New Year is celebrated in almost every part of the world. However, the nature, duration and time of celebration may vary greatly from country to country. For example, the date of Chinese Lunar New Year or Spring Festival varies every year; while in Mexico, the two-week period including Christmas and New Year's Day is not a good time to conduct business nor is the two-week period prior to Easter, as businesspeople are usually traveling with their families during this time.

For most Arabs, Ramadan is the holy month every year. Little business is conducted during this month. In Japan, many companies close from April 29 to May 5 to celebrate various holidays and birthdays.

Key Term

holiday 节假日

中国的传统节日与中国的传统历法、农耕社会密切相关，同时较为注重家庭与和谐。西方的节日更多是表现人们的互动性、集体性和狂欢性，以自我为中心，崇尚个性张扬。

Glossary

carnival	*n.*	狂欢节；嘉年华会；饮宴狂欢
Catholic	*adj.*	天主教的
	n.	天主教教徒
firework	*n.*	烟火；激烈情绪
holy	*adj.*	圣洁的；神圣的；至善的
	n.	神圣的东西
observance	*n.*	惯例；遵守；仪式；庆祝
parade	*n.*	游行；阅兵；行进；阅兵场

picnic	*n.* 野餐	
	vi. 去野餐	
Sabbath	*n.* 安息日	

Comprehension Questions

1. How do business persons spend holidays or holy days in overseas countries?
2. What are the differences to celebrate holidays or holy days across different cultures?

4. Bribery 贿赂

Bribery is the act of offering someone money or something valuable in order to persuade them to do something for you. In the past few years, bribery has undergone close scrutiny and is considered unethical and immoral in many countries. Some countries have established laws to fight against bribery, for example, America has the most restrictive laws against bribery. In America, companies found guilty of paying bribes to foreign officials can be fined up to $1 million, and guilty employees may be fined up to $10,000 (Engholm, 1991).

Although bribery is officially sanctioned or not condoned in any country, it is unofficially a part of business in some cultures. In Nigeria, a person must pay the customs agent in order to leave the airport; in Thailand and Indonesia, getting a driver's license involves giving a tip to an agent (Engholm & Rowland, 1996). According to Indonesians, bribery saves time and effort when dealing with top officials who make final decisions. In this country business people have found that bribing a top government official to get a big contract is far less time-consuming than preparing a good proposal for bidding (Hodge, 2000).

What's important for businesspeople to notice is that once your business becomes globalized, some situations that are considered illegal in your own countries may not be unlawful in some other countries; sometimes these situations are even accepted part of doing business.

Key Term

bribery 贿赂

送礼是贿赂的一种。为什么要送礼？送什么礼？如何送礼？对这些问题的回答要视具体情况而定。这些情况包括送礼的原因和目的、送礼的对象和时间。由于存在文化差异的问题，在跨文化交际中，送礼问题更加复杂。

Glossary

bidding	*n.* 投标；出价；命令
bribe	*vt.* 贿赂；收买
bribery	*n.* 贿赂；受贿；行贿
immoral	*adj.* 不道德的；邪恶的；淫荡的
Indonesian	*n.* 印尼人；印尼语群；印度尼西亚语
restrictive	*adj.* 限制的；限制性的；约束的
scrutiny	*n.* 详细审查；监视；细看；选票复查
unethical	*adj.* 不道德的；缺乏职业道德的

Comprehension Questions

1. What is bribery?
2. What measures do you know the countries take to deal with bribery?

5. Business Card Exchange 交换名片

An important aspect of business protocol is the proper procedure for exchanging business cards. Conventionally, a business card may include information like the company's name and logo, one's name, rank, title, profession, e-mail, telephone, fax and foreign headquarters where appropriate. In non-English speaking countries, have the information on your card printed in English on one side and in the local language on the other.

The right timing for card exchange is important in business contact. Exchanging cards during the first meeting with others is considered appropriate and decent, which means mutual intention of further contact. When meeting with foreign business people, it is better to prepare a bilingual card and present it with the target language translation side up. Do prepare enough cards for potential business partners, but do not give out your cards randomly for it may not be taken seriously. The better thing to do is to decide whether there are possibilities for further contact and future business before exchange your card with others. Exchange your card privately at parties or where there are a lot of people and never give out your cards like poker cards to everyone present. Make sure your cards are easy to reach when you are about to exchange with others. Be polite when you want to meet someone and ask for his card, or your cards are running out: “May I have your card please?” “This is my card, and please call me if there is need.” “I am sorry I have sent out all my cards.” or “Sorry I have no cards on me today.”

In different cultures and countries, people present their cards differently. In the United States, it might be normal for people to glance at the card they get and put it away promptly in the pocket. Whereas in Japan, this behavior can be considered very rude, for Japanese people consider it polite to examine the card carefully and make some comments before they put it away. Besides, Japanese as well as Koreans present their card with both their hands, so it is better for foreigners to do in the same way. In Northern Europe, people are respectful of age, so include your company's date of establishment on your business card when the company's history is a long one (Turkington, 1999). Australian business persons do not usually carry business cards; thus, when you offer them your card, you may not receive one in return. In Latin American countries, business titles are important, so be sure to include them on your business cards (Moran et al., 2011).

Key Term

business card exchange 交换名片

交换名片时需要注意一些礼仪。在出席商务活动的时候，一般都会交换名片，交换名片能看出对对方的重视程度和个人修养情况。

Glossary

bilingual	*adj.* 双语的	
	n. 通两种语言的人	
headquarter	*vi.* 设立总部	
	vt. 在……设总部	
mutual	*adj.* 共同的；相互的；彼此的	
randomly	*adv.* 随便地；任意地；无目的地；未加计划地	

Comprehension Questions

1. Is there something common in exchanging business card among different cultures? If the answer is yes, then what is it?
2. What are the differences in exchanging business card among different cultures?

6. Position and Status 社会地位和职位

Acknowledgment of the attendees' social status and their corresponding positions may show them proper respect, avoid unnecessary misunderstanding and embarrassment, and contribute to the success of intercultural communication encounters. Definitions of social class vary greatly from country to country and culture to culture. People in different parts of the world have their own distinct way of identifying the classes.

Although class distinctions in some countries are more subtle than others, social equality is not absolute in any countries. For example, Americans show less respect for rank and authority than the people in some European countries like Great Britain or some Asian countries. It is easy for foreigners to miss the existence of a class structure and mistakenly believe that distinctions in position do not exist in this country. However, the truth is Americans may not inherit titles and ranks like the British hereditary system of nobility where certain factors distinguish between the top social class, the middle social class, and the lower social class. Visitors to New York, Washington D.C. and other cities, however, may see both the homeless and more affluent persons in public places.

In some Asian countries, more rigid social system exists. For example, a caste is one of the traditional social classes into which people are divided in a Hindu society. The particular caste a person belongs to is determined at birth; each caste system has its status, rights, and duties. Although discrimination based on caste has been outlawed, in many areas, particularly rural ones, it is still a major influence on life in India. In India's rigid caste system, interaction between members of different castes is often limited, as in the case of India's untouchables (Samovar & Porter, 2003).

Inequality between men and women still exists in some countries. In Republic of Korea, women are considered inferior to men and thus have lower social status. Women, even those with college degrees, are rarely employed as executives. In Malaysia and Singapore, men are clearly the ones in positions of authority (Chaney & Martin, 2007; Turkington, 1999). Similarly in Mexico, women in companies may not receive the same respect given to men with the same positions. But this cannot deny the progress made in the process of striving for the equality between male and female. In Arab countries, social status of women has been improving. More women have begun to hold positions of executives in companies.

In China, age is greatly respected. Age is viewed as an indication of seniority, and advanced years can represent wisdom and respect. In China and Japan, ranks of people are also important. When entering a room, they generally enter in protocol order, with the highest-ranking person entering first. They will also assume that the first member of your negotiating team to enter the room is the head of your group or has the higher rank. Sitting in rank order during a meeting, negotiation, or dinner can only be regarded as acceptable (Axtell, 1998; Turkington, 1999). And to Japanese, it is customary for people of lower rank to bow first and lowest to the higher rank.

Key Term

position and status 社会地位和职位

在跨文化交际中，了解交际对象的社会地位和相应的职位可能会避免交际中不必要的误解和尴尬，有助于跨文化交流的成功。有些国家的阶层差别比其他国家更为微妙，总而言之，社会平等是一个相对概念，具有不同的文化内涵。

Glossary

acknowledgment	*n.* 感谢；承认；承认书
Arabian	*adj.* 阿拉伯的；阿拉伯人的
	n. 阿拉伯人
attendee	*n.* 出席者；在场者
caste	*n.*（印度社会中的）种姓
embarrassment	*n.* 窘迫；难堪；使人为难的人或事物
executive	*adj.* 行政的；经营的；经营管理的
	n. 管理人员；领导层
inequality	*n.* 不平等；不同；不平均
inferior	*adj.* 差的；自卑的；下级的；下等的
inherit	*vt.* 继承；遗传而得
mistakenly	*adv.* 错误地；曲解地；被误解地
protocol	*n.* 协议；草案；礼仪
rigid	*adj.* 严格的；僵硬的，死板的
seniority	*n.* 长辈；老资格；前任者的特权
untouchable	*n.* 贱民；被遗弃的人

Comprehension Question

What are the positions and status of business persons in different cultures?

7. Electronic Communication Etiquette 电子交流礼仪

Electronic communication may include the telephone calls and cyber communication. Good telephone manners and following rules of online communication may avoid unnecessary embarrassment and misunderstanding and help enhance credibility.

7.1 Telephone Communication 电话交流

The biggest problems with telephone communication are that people cannot make a deep impression by the objective conditions like the size of one's office, one's decent dressing, etc. The only way to leave a good impression is through your voice and attitude. Therefore, telephone manners are especially important when one wants to establish long distance business relationship and expand further cooperation. Here are some rules of good telephone manners to follow:

Answer the phone promptly. It is considered good manner and appropriate to pick up the phone before the third ring. Answering phones promptly makes people appreciate your consideration of valuing the caller's time. If one fails to answer promptly after several rings, a polite apology like "sorry to keep you waiting" is appropriate, because the caller will never know what keeps you busy at the moment of calling; all they learn is that their phones are delayed. Answering phones promptly can no doubt help build credibility for your company.

Inform the caller of your identity and company, even on mobile phones. Phones from external line require you to inform the caller of the name of your company and your identity, while phones from internal lines may only need you to inform of your title and department. In doing so, efficiency can be guaranteed and a good impression of professionalism can be left.

Ask for some relevant information at first. After informing the caller of one's basic information, one should ask for basic information like the caller's company, name, title, etc., and try to remember clearly for further contact.

Listen to the caller carefully. When answering the phone, it is better to stop other things one is doing at the moment, learn about the caller's questions and needs carefully, and take note about some important information for future reference. It is recommended to prepare telephone directory, notebook and pen beside the phone. Never answer the phone with a full mouth of food. Keep one's voice lively and the tone a little bit up. When listening to the caller's talking, respond with something positive like "yes" "uh-huh", etc. accordingly from time to time so that the caller may know he or she is being carefully listened to. Do not interrupt the caller. When there is an emergency or it is not convenient to talk at the moment, inform the caller politely and tell him or her that you will call back soon. Return the calls you miss as soon as possible no matter whether the caller requires a call back, and apologize when it is delayed for a long time with a good explanation.

Repeat the main content of the call before hang up the phone. Except for a note of some important information, it is necessary to repeat what you have discussed over the phone, especially some significant information like date, number, place, etc., for a double check so that mistakes can be avoided at the beginning.

Hang up the phone politely. Normally, it is customary for the caller to hang up first. Do not hang up hastily even before the caller finishes talking. At the end of the phone call, it is appropriate to extend courtesy by saying some polite remarks like "thanks for calling" "good bye", etc.

7.2 E-mail Communication 电子邮件交流

Since e-mails through internet have almost replaced ordinary mails nowadays, the communication etiquette other than telephone calls mainly refer to e-mail etiquette.

When sending an e-mail to a business partner, it is important to follow some basic rules. First, it's better to send your e-mail with a proper theme in the subject line rather than with some casual words like "Hi" or "Hello" so that the receiver would know the general idea immediately. Second, like traditional mails, e-mail also needs to be concise and clear. Check for spelling mistakes, unnecessary lines as well as the format before send it out. Third, send twice the very important e-mail to make sure the receiver gets it, or call the receiver after you send it to remind him or her to check the e-mail box in time. Fourth, try to reply every e-mail you receive as soon as possible.

7.3 Traditional Letter Communication 传统书信交流

Even though people seldom send paper mails these days, traditional mails may also play an important role in doing business. For example, invitation letters, reminder cards, thank-you cards, complaint letters as well as replies to these letters and cards are all indispensible even in today's world. As business correspondence acts like a tool for business communication which is also legally valid at the same time, business letter etiquette is worthy of proper attention. The first thing about traditional letters is the format. Usually business letters should use particular letter papers with the company's letterhead on it which should also be of high quality. Secondly, the appellation should be appropriate. If no information about the sex of the receiver could be required, use his or her title instead of Ms. or Mr. Thirdly, try to make sure your handwriting is beautiful, your language is clear and fluent and your attitude is polite, all of which will help leave a good impression to the receiver. The diction should also be formal rather than rare and obscure. Your tone should be sincere and natural, but not be too colloquial as well.

Key Term

electronic communication 电子交流

电子交流可以包括电话、电报、邮件、微信、QQ，甚至微博等网络通信。电子交流是现代商业社会的一种主要联络手段，其礼仪方式有别于传统的商业交流。

Glossary

casual	*adj.* 随便的；非正式的；临时的；偶然的
credibility	*n.* 可信性；确实性
colloquial	*adj.* 白话的；通俗的；口语体的
courtesy	*n.* 礼貌；好意；恩惠
diction	*n.* 用语；措辞
enhance	*vt.* 提高；加强；增加
indispensable	*adj.* 不可缺少的；绝对必要的；责无旁贷的
promptly	*adv.* 迅速地；立即地；敏捷地

Comprehension Question

What is electronic communication etiquette?

8. Dining Practices 餐桌礼仪

Roughly speaking, the eating styles of the world can be divided into several types, for example, the Asian type, the American type, the European type and others including Africa and other places, even though in all these places, specific dining practices may also vary greatly.

8.1 Asian Type 亚洲餐桌礼仪

In many parts of Asia, people usually use chopsticks rather than knives and forks. Chopsticks are placed on the chopstick rest at the conclusion of the meal (or when pausing during the meal); they should not be placed in an upright position in the rice bowl (Martin & Chaney, 2012; Sabath, 2002). In Japan, people would dine sitting in a kneeling position on a tatami mat. If you have frequent contact with Japanese, practicing this art is warranted (Axtell, 1993).

8.2 American Type 美国餐桌礼仪

American dining practices actually differ greatly from Europe. For example, the main meal in America is in the evening instead of noon. What's more different from Europeans is that Americans prefer a business meeting during breakfast time. Another US business custom questioned by people in other cultures is the lengthy cocktail "hour" before dinner. Italians have commented that the endless rounds of cocktails before ordering a meal are exhausting and may result in discussions that make little sense (Baldrige, 1993; Martin & Chaney, 2012).

8.3 European Type 欧洲餐桌礼仪

While in European countries, dining practices are also different. For example, unlike America, countries like Italy and France, salads are served after the main course. In America, dinner usually opens from 5 to 7 in the afternoon, whereas in Spain, dinner can be late till 10 o'clock in the evening. In France, people would never have meetings during breakfast like Americans do; they usually have business lunches instead. Even with those differences, European countries still follow a common eating style called the Continental eating style. Actually Europeans ate in the same way with Americans until around 1850, and then the

European upper class began to use the forks and knives differently, with the fork always in the left and the knife in the right hand. They use the knife to push food onto the back of the fork, and then move the food into the mouth with the tines of the fork down.

8.4 Dining Practices in Other Cultures and Attentions 其他地区餐桌礼仪文化及注意事项

There are other dining practices in other parts of the world. For example, in Latin America, even informal meals have numerous courses. In Mexico, lunch time varies from 2 to 4 o'clock in the afternoon. In Middle East, people usually eat with their right hand, the same is true with Tahiti.

When entertaining visitors from other countries, be considerate and ask them whether they prefer the main meal at noon or in the evening and take them to restaurants where they have a choice of a light or heavy meal (Devine & Braganti, 2000; Martin & Chaney, 2012). When the dinner is open, there are several rules to follow so that one can eat gracefully. First is the posture. One needs to sit up straight and keeps the elbows off the table. Second is the right time to eat. Only when everyone has been served and the host and/or hostess begin to eat can one begin to follow. Then it is the right way to eat. In American dining style, one can cut a few bites (usually no more than three bites) at a time and place the knife across the top of the plate with the sharp edge towards oneself, and then switch the fork from the left hand to the right with the tines up to bring the food into the mouth. While in European eating style, one can only cut one bite at a time and use the fork in the left hand with the tines pointing down to spear the food and bring it into the mouth.

Key Term

dining practices 餐桌礼仪

中西餐桌礼仪在跨文化方面有餐具使用差异、座次安排差异、就餐氛围差异及餐桌话语差异等，旨在说明坚持自己的优秀文化传统的同时，要采用一个客观、宽容、尊重的心态对待异国文化，以便能在跨文化交际中恰当地、得体地进行交际。

Glossary

cocktail	*n.* 鸡尾酒；开胃食品
continental	*adj.* 大陆的；大陆性的

gracefully	*adv.*	优雅地；温文地
posture	*n.*	姿势；态度；情形
warranted	*adj.*	保证的；担保的

Comprehension Questions

1. What are the features of dining practices in Asia, America and Europe?
2. How do the dining practices vary from culture to culture?

9. Tipping 服务小费

In countries like the United States and European countries, tipping is customary practice, which is considered a reward for the services performed by the service people. While in some other countries, tipping is not well accepted, for example in Japan, Singapore, etc. In cultures like these, tipping is just expected and may even be considered offence.

In those tipping-favored countries, it is very hard to set definite rules for tips. Tipping can differ from country to country and business to business. What's more, the services being offered can also be good or bad. However, even if one is very unsatisfied with the services he or she receives, leaving a few coins is not accepted, for it is called insulting tipping, which shows a lack of respect. Therefore, in almost all service industries, a tip is always merited, especially when the service is good. Normally, 15% to 20% of the bill is considered a well-accepted amount of tips. But 20% is now closer to the norm since trends in tipping have been changing in the past few years.

Common situations that require tipping may include traveling, dining in fancy restaurants, summoning cabs, etc. For example, when traveling, you may encounter numerous situations where you may feel things all go smoothly if you have a supply of 1 dollar bills or 5 dollar bills in your pocket. These may include tipping for the cab driver who drives you to the hotel, the bellboy who helps you with the luggage when you are checking in and other service personnel who perform room services, like delivering food to your room, etc. Travel tipping needs to be included in anticipated travel expenses; tipping service personnel at a resort or luxury hotel may add an additional 25% to your bill (Chaney & Martin, 2007; Martin & Chaney, 2012).

Even though tipping is very commonly conducted, it is better to know one or two things before going to these tipping-favored countries especially when you are a foreigner from a non-tipping culture. Firstly, you are supposed to offer more tips when the service is provided longer or better. Secondly, do not give too much more than necessary, otherwise you may be considered foolish. For those most commonly seen lines of work that receive tips as an important part of income, there are still general rules to follow. For cab drivers, 15% to 20% of the fare is the norm; additional tip is expected for carrying heavy bags. For porters, one or two dollars is usually tipped. For parking attendants, one dollar is tipped for bringing your car. For cloakroom attendants, one dollar is given for one coat. For waiters, 15% to 20% of the bill is commonly accepted, including tax. 25% is the top. For bartenders, 15% to 20% of the bill is common, with a minimum of 50 cents.

However, in those countries that do not see tipping as a customary behavior, it is better to learn something in case of embarrassment. For example, a thanks letter may be much more appreciated than tips when you receive great help in hotels. Japanese people do not like being tipped for they believe their help is just a gesture of hospitality and tips can be seen as offence. If you do feel that someone deserves a reward for his extra or her services, you can put the tips in an envelope for the Japanese people believe receiving money openly is embarrassing. Likewise in Singapore and Republic of Korea, tipping is not expected, although this practice seems to be changing in hotels where international businesspersons stay (Martin & Chaney, 2012).

Key Term

tipping 服务小费

在交际过程中，非语言因素占据着重要的位置。每个国家给小费的风俗习惯不同，这就要求我们注意跨文化交际中的非语言因素，注重自身能力的提升。

Glossary

attendant	*n.* 服务员；侍者；随员；陪从
bellboy	*n.* 侍者
fancy	*n.* 幻想；想象力；爱好
hospitality	*n.* 好客；殷勤
merited	*adj.* 应得的；理所当然的
offence	*n.* 犯罪；违反；过错；攻击
summoning	*n.* 召唤
tip	*n.* 小费

Comprehension Question

What situations require tipping?

Extended Activities

Case Analysis

Case 1

Liu Zhong is the President of a multi-national company (MNC). He brought the Secretary Wang and his entourage to Iran to participate in the final business negotiations for exporting a group of electronic machines. Liu Zhong and his group arrived in Iran on the afternoon of the day to visit the company, when it happened to canonical hour. The host indicated that they were waiting for further talks. But Liu Zhong felt a little dissatisfied with such an arrangement for it didn't work efficiently. The host expressed his welcome to this visiting group and held a welcome party. Secretary Wang hoped to dress on the simple and refined clothes to show the Chinese women's wisdom, beauty and generosity. She was wearing a white and tight sleeveless shirt and a blue skirt. Strange sights was cast on her in the whole party. The owner gave drinks to each Chinese guest. When Miss Wang used her left hand to hold the drink habitually, the owner immediately changed the face and then impolitely put the drink on the table. What made Liu Zhong and his entourage confused was that in the next talks the host who had always been very sincere for the cooperation had no longer any substantive talks with them.

(Adapted from: Dou Ran. International Business Negotiation[M]. Shanghai: Fudan University Press, 2008.)

Questions for Discussion

1. What are the main differences in business etiquette and customs between Chinese business persons and Iranian business persons?
2. Why do the two parties have no longer substantive talks?

Case 2

Wang Jin, the director of a Foreign Economic and Trade Commission, was sent with a delegation to visit Europe for the investment work. Because before she went abroad and forgot to re-print a business card, so every time she sent business cards, in order to show their latest phone and address, she corrected quickly on the business card with a pen temporarily and added a few of useful phone numbers and addresses. Half a month later, Ms. Wang tired exhaustedly, but no foreign had the substantive contact with her, and later on others pointed out what the problem was originally turned out to be, she understood. The reason was that her own business card was offensive to the established foreign business norms. To solve the problem, Ms. Wang added a few useful phone numbers temporarily with a pen on their own business cards, and her original intention was to contact more conveniently and more effectively, but in the view of foreigners, business card is a person's "face". Its arbitrary change and correction can only show her perfunctory in business matters.

(Source: Chaney L H, Martin J S. The Essential Guide to Business Etiquette[M]. New York: Praeger Press, 2007.)

Questions for Discussion

1. Try to talk about the important role in business cards for today's business contacts combined with Ms. Wang's mistakes.
2. Please think about how to show business cards correctly.

Further Reading

Business Etiquette

Janusz Świerkocki

1.1 What Is Etiquette and Why Do You Need to Know and Observe It?

The word "etiquette" in the context of this discussion means "the rules of behavior standard in polite society" (*The New Lexicon*, 1988). Commonly, etiquette is interpreted as good manners, which may apply to various social settings with the business setting being one of the most important. The latter is also an ambiguous term that for the needs of further considerations will be understood as a "workplace", within which, and in relation to which, we establish relationships with other actors of economic transactions. It may be an enterprise, an office or a law firm, but also a public institution, research center or university. The staff and clients of all these establishments should exhibit good manners.

By following etiquette, we show respect to others. Such an attitude serves well the interests of employers and employees as, on the one hand, it is relevant for the smooth operation of each and every institution and, on the other hand, it facilitates a successful professional career. Firstly, mutual respect favors a good organizational atmosphere which is vital for the commitment of employees, their honesty, proper time management and identification with the firm, etc. Such attitudes impact reasonable use of the raw materials, materials, machinery and knowledge that the organization possesses. The good manners of the employees may attract clients more easily and encourage them to stay instead of choosing competitors. Consequently, the market position of an organization gets reinforced. Secondly, practicing etiquette boosts your self-confidence. When you know how to behave in a particular setting, you are more relaxed and can better focus on substantive issues. Thirdly, observing etiquette is a way to be respectful and trustful in the eyes of other people, which helps in professional development although, obviously, we must remember that having good manners does not necessarily go hand in hand with professionalism and high moral standards.

According to sociologists, good manners belong to social norms while economists category them as informal institutions. They originate from tradition, culture and customs and are neither codified nor written down. Manners provide a code of conduct and tell us what to do and what not to do in various social settings. Usually, they concur with the norms that regulate the lives of individual communities (legal, moral) but sometimes they contradict them. For example, while legal and moral norms impose the duty of truth telling, a comment addressed to a co-worker who takes little care of their personal hygiene may be a reason for a decline in mutual relations. Not observing etiquette often means committing faux pas. Although that itself does not imply legal sanctions, sometimes not even reprehension by others, the act may have unpleasant consequences, such as critical remarks, being ridiculed, embarrassed or looked down on by colleagues. That is why one should not ignore or disregard etiquette.

Due to their origin, good manners are general or universal only to a very limited extent. In most cases their scope is limited by place, time and social environment. Discussing them all would be a near to impossible task. Punctuality, for example, is understood differently in countries of Latin America and in Anglo-Saxon countries; a visiting card was once used when paying visits while nowadays it does not perform this role any more; addressing others by their first names is natural among students, but less popular among slightly older people. These rules evolve. Dress codes have become more flexible in recent years. Technical progress has also brought new rules, like those connected with using mobile phones or e-mails.

Considering the above circumstances, one may say that, firstly, we should be flexible in our approach to good manners and show understanding for cultural differences; and secondly, it is simply impossible to learn business etiquette in full. In fact, both comments are correct. Nevertheless, one should at least try to learn as many rules as possible which will facilitate making a good impression in dealings with business partners. It is especially true when meeting people from other countries. One should also bear in mind that changes and new phenomena are true of the forms rather than of the building blocks of etiquette. The latter are stable and can be best illustrated by the old Polish saying "do as you would be done by".

1.2 Greeting Someone and Saying Hello, Saying Goodbye

Greeting someone and saying hello are the first opportunity for personal contact which makes a lasting impression on interlocutors, often decisive for further relations between the parties involved. When meeting people you already know, both are usually automatic, you do not analyze why they take one form or another. But when it comes to people you do not know, the issue requires a little more attention and taking account of various circumstances.

Greetings come in two forms: verbal, which is mandatory, and nonverbal, which does not always accompany the first one. There are some differences between the two which are worth highlighting to avoid misunderstandings. They are connected with the principle of precedence.

The verbal part of a greeting is a greeting phrase. It may take various forms. If you know the other person sufficiently well, you may say, e.g., "Hello". In other cases you usually say "Good morning (Good afternoon, Good evening)". If you want to sound more polite, you may personalize the greeting by saying, e.g., "Good morning, Madam" "Good morning, Doctor" "Good Morning, Madam Director", etc. In some languages (French, English) you may also add the person's last name, but in Polish culture addressing someone by saying "Good morning, Mr. X" is not in good taste and may be considered offensive.

Etiquette strictly requires us to greet people we know and respond to greetings of others without any exception. When it comes to precedence, in accordance with the principle universally acknowledged in everyday life, the relationship of the status of the two people, referred to as seniority in etiquette, decides. The person of lower status always greets first, i.e., a man greets a woman; a younger person greets an older person; a student greets a professor, etc. Things get more complicated when the dividing lines are not exclusive and a younger woman meets an older man. In business, the principle is easier, precedence is based on hierarchy, i.e., sex or age is irrelevant. Thus, a female employee should greet her superior first and a shop-assistant should greet her/his client independently of how old they are. However, also in these cases some doubts may arise, especially when age differences are substantial, e.g., a woman who is a shop assistant who is much older than her male client. All these complexities should be dispelled by the use of common sense: there is nothing wrong in a superior greeting his employees first. This is one of the cases to which an old principle applies, according to which the more polite of the two says "Good morning" first.

It may also happen that a particular setting takes precedence over seniority. And thus:

- people inside a room (conference room, classroom, waiting room, reception, on-call room, lift, etc.) should no doubt be greeted by those who enter;
- people who are standing (in the corridor, on the pavement, etc.) should be greeted by those who are walking (riding).

A non-verbal element of greeting is, depending on the circumstances, a bow, a nod, tipping a hat, a kiss but most often a handshake. And the precedence here is the reverse to the one for verbal greetings. Customarily, a woman extends her hand first to a man, an older person to a younger, a professor to a student, etc. A similar sequence applies to saying goodbye. However, in business settings, the rules are suspended, making room for hierarchy. Hence, it is appropriate when a younger director extends his hand to an older employee or to a female receptionist. When ranks are equal, it does not matter who does it first, the man or the woman (but a host should do it first to a guest). Unlike when saying hello, in doubtful situations, especially at the beginning of an acquaintance, it is worth remaining slightly reserved and not extending a hand first.

Extending a hand in itself is almost instinctive and we do not always pay attention to how we do it. Hence, we should, first and foremost, remember that:

- The palm must be clean and dry (something to be remembered, e.g., when you are holding a glass with cold drink at a party, as the hand gets damp);
- When extending the hand, you should briefly make eye contact with the other person (in some cultures, e.g., in Japan, this is not practiced).

Depending on the circumstances, it is nice to include a pleasantry (e.g., when we have not seen each other for a longer period or this is the first meeting ever):

- The palm should be held perpendicular to the floor (some people, women in particular, extend the hand parallel, "covering" the palm of the partner);
- You do not want to offer a limp hand "to be held", but you offer a firm grip, not overpowering and not too long;
- The refusal of a handshake is a serious insult to the other person;
- In the workplace, you do not have to shake hands every day but you should do it after, e.g., a longer period away.

To finish the subject of saying hello, it is necessary to comment on hand-kissing. This custom, still alive in Poland and also practiced in, e.g., France, provokes no embarrassment in private relationships but it does not fit business and official contacts although some women tend to extend their hands in a way suggesting that they simply expect the gesture from the man. Thus, remember that in official relations:

- If you want to practice this form of courtesy, you should kiss the hands of all women at a particular gathering, not only some of them (depending on the age, position, appearance or any other criteria);
- You should not do it in a hurry, mechanically, by dragging the hand up to your lips (which, as we can sometimes see on TV, some politicians do) but you should bow a little;
- The custom does not match situations such as receiving awards, diplomas, nominations and also, as once playfully observed by Ambassador Pietkiewicz, fines for the infringement of traffic rules (Pietkiewicz, 1998, p103).

Saying goodbye, similar to saying hello, may also consist of two parts: verbal and non-verbal. The only difference is that it is initiated by the person in the higher position of authority (someone older, a superior, a woman) by saying, e.g., "Goodbye" and possibly extending a hand.

(Source: Tomasz Doro yński, Janusz wierkocki. Practical Aspects in Doing International Business[M]. Krakow: Wydawnictwo Uniwersytetu Łódzkieg, 2016.)

Unit 7 Business Negotiation across Cultures

Learning Objectives

After learning this unit, you will be able to:

- ✧ define negotiation and intercultural business negotiation;
- ✧ understand the influence of cultural differences on negotiation;
- ✧ understand negotiation strategies;
- ✧ identify the phases of negotiation.

Warm-up

1. How are business negotiations across cultures different from domestic ones?
2. Use examples to explain the cultural differences in business negotiation.

Focused Study

1. Influence of Cultural Differences on Negotiation 文化差异对谈判的影响

The word "negotiation" derives from the Roman word "negotiari" which means "to do business or trade". It can be defined as a process of coordinating common interests and resolving conflicting issues between the parties involved.

Intercultural business negotiation is one that takes place between the interest groups from different countries or regions. Intercultural negotiations are far more complex than domestic ones since more factors should be put into consideration, such as culture, legal and political systems, the exchange value of international currencies, government regulations, social and political instability, ideology, external stakeholders, etc.

In intercultural business negotiations, it is natural that each party tends to orient their strategies and interests around their own culture. However, effective negotiations require the negotiators to understand cultural differences in negotiation attitudes, behaviours and contexts. Weiss and Stripp (1998) proposed the following 12 variables that should be taken into consideration in the negotiation process.

1.1 Basic Conception of Negotiations 谈判的基本观念

Culture influences the way people view a negotiation as distributive or integrative.

A distributive (also known as strategic) negotiation is often referred to as a "win-lose" or "fixed-pie". It is construed as a competitive process of offers and counter-offers in which the interests of the parties are directly in conflict. The negotiators try to maximize their own goals and interests, seeing one party's gains as the other's losses. Negotiators in the United States, for example, are predisposed to view negotiation as being fundamentally distributive.

An integrative (also known as synergistic) negotiation is often referred to as a "win-win" and involves a process that integrates the goals of the parties involved. The negotiators tend to understand the underlying issues and their relative importance to both parties, aiming to capitalize on the different interests of each party so as to find satisfactory trade-offs. Negotiators in some European countries and Asian countries tend to be integrative in negotiation.

1.2 Types of Issue 事务类型

Basically four types of issues may arise during business negotiations: task-based, relationship-based, procedural, and personal/internal. Negotiators from different cultures tend to spend more time on different types of issues in discussion, especially the first two types.

Negotiators who stress task issues tend to focus on specific operational details and information exchange. Negotiators from the United States are typically task-based. German negotiators are generally regarded as poor conversation partners since they see no point in small talk.

In contrast, negotiators from cultures where relationship-based issues are more important tend to focus on the relationship between the two parties. Considerable time is spent on establishing rapport between the members. It's important to build trust and friendship before the discussion of task issues. Some Asian countries such as China and Japan are more relationship-based since they tend to link both success and advancement with relationship. The French also put emphasis on personal relations in establishing solid business cooperation.

1.3 Selection of Negotiators 谈判人员的选择

The criteria that are used to select who will participate in a negotiation are different across cultures. These criteria may include negotiating experience, knowledge of the subject matter being negotiated, seniority, political affiliation, family connections, gender, age, and other personal attributes such as affability, loyalty and trustworthiness in the eyes of the principal. Different cultures weigh these criteria differently. Therefore, expectations about what is appropriate in negotiations may vary in different cultures.

These criteria can be roughly divided into two groups: abilities and status. In some Western cultures such as the United States and Canada, negotiation teams are largely made up of technical advisers and people that have demonstrated proficiency in the project. In some other cultures like France and Mexico, negotiation teams are largely made up of senior and high-ranking officials who exert great influence on their organizations.

Case 1

Sending whiz-kids to deal with people 10 to 20 years their senior often insults the ascriptive culture. The reaction may be: "Do these people think they have reached our own level of experience in half the time? That a 30-year-old American is good enough to negotiate with a 50-year-old Greek or Italian?" Achievement cultures must understand that some ascriptive cultures, Japanese especially, spend much on training and in-house education to ensure that older people actually are wiser for the years they have spent in the corporation and for the sheer number of subordinates briefing them. It insults an ascriptive culture to do anything which prevents the self-fulfilling nature of its beliefs. Older people are held to be important so that they will be nourished and sustained by others' respect. A stranger is expected to facilitate this scheme, not challenge it.

(Source: Luthans F, Jonathan D. International Management: Culture, Strategy and Behavior [M]. London: McGraw-Hill Education, 2014.)

1.4 Influence of Individual Aspirations 个人愿望的影响

The emphasis negotiators place on their individual goals and needs for recognition may also vary in different cultures. Negotiators from individualistic societies such as the United States are emotionally independent from the organization which they work for. Although they also keep the organization's interests and goals in mind, the negotiators mainly strive to gain personal reward and recognition for their decisions in the negotiation.

On the other hand, negotiators from collectivist cultures such as Japan regard organizational gains to be more important than personal recognition. They have a strong sense of identity with and loyalty to the group they belong to. Therefore, they will give more consideration to the group interests without expectation of personal gain or recognition.

1.5 Internal Decision-making Process 内部决策过程

This variable refers to the system by which negotiators reach decisions within their teams, and between their teams and the organization they represent. Generally speaking, decision-making system can be divided into two types: authoritative or consensual.

In authoritative decision-making cultures, decisions are made independently by individuals without considering the viewpoints of other members on the team or consulting with their superiors on the team. The United States is such an individual-oriented culture, where being independent and assertive is valued and praised.

In contrast, negotiators from consensus decision-making cultures do not have the authority to make decisions unless they consult the other members on the team. Negotiators from countries like Japan are more interdependent within the team and tend to make decisions collectively. German negotiators are also slow at making decisions since they have a consensus decision-making process.

1.6 Orientation toward Time 时间取向

Cultures have different views on what time means and how it affects negotiations. There are basically two types of time orientation: monochronic or polychronic.

Monochronic cultures emphasize making agendas for meetings and being on time for appointments. In Japan, America and Germany, for example, time is valued and delay is particularly irritating. People tend to appear for meetings at an appointed hour, being sensitive to not wasting others' time.

In contrast, polychronic cultures stress the involvement of people rather than preset schedules. Negotiators from these cultures tend to integrate task-oriented activities with socio-emotional ones. Some countries from Latin America and Asia often take polychronic orientation to time. The pace in these countries is much slower. In these cultures, time is not important. The focus is on the task, regardless of the amount of time it takes.

Case 2

On his first trip to Cancun (a city in Mexico), Liu Zhong, a marketing manager of a Chinese importing and exporting company who intended to negotiate a contract with a local firm, was invited to a dinner party by his Mexican counterpart. Since the invitation indicated that cocktails would begin at 6:30 p.m., Liu Zhong arrived on that very time. His host seemed surprised, and no one else had arrived. People began arriving about 7:30 p.m. Liu Zhong knew he had read the invitation correctly but felt he had gotten off to a bad start.

(Adapted from: 庄恩平. 跨文化商务沟通教程：阅读与案例[M]. 上海：上海外语教育出版社，2014.)

1.7 Risk Propensity 风险倾向

Cultures vary in the extent to which they are willing to take risks. Negotiators in risk-avoiding cultures may be reluctant to approve proposals whose success is linked to unknowns and contingencies. They tend to have bureaucratic, conservative decision makers who want a great deal of information before making decision. Some European cultures, for example Germany, are quite conservative and tend to make good preparations.

In contrast, risk-tolerant negotiators hold that there is a level of acceptable risk that should be taken in a negotiation. The negotiators are more entrepreneurial and willing to take risks when they have incomplete information. They are also more willing to take the risk of failing to reach an agreement. The United States and some Asian cultures are generally believed to fall on the risk-taking end in negotiations.

1.8 Bases of Trust 信任的基础

Trust is one party's confidence in the other party's reliability and integrity. Trust is important in all cultures and provides the foundation on which both parties can work together in a negotiation. However, business negotiators trust each other for different reasons, which can be external or internal.

In some cultures negotiators trust the other party because there is a signed contract and the sanction of law to support it. This kind of trust is external to both parties. Both parties will honor the terms of the contract because the legal system will impose sanctions otherwise.

In contrast, in other cultures negotiators trust the other party because of the friendly relationship that exists between them. This kind of trust is internal to the relationship. The relationship is much more important than the contract, which is only a symbol of the bond between the parties who drafted it.

1.9 Concern with Protocol 对礼仪的重视

Concern with protocol has to do with the importance placed on the existence of and adherence to rules for acceptable self-presentation and social behavior such as the international courtesies of business.

Cultures differ in the degree to which protocol, or the formality of the relations between the two negotiating parties. Negotiators from formal cultures are highly concerned with negotiation etiquette. They will adhere to negotiating procedures and rules that govern personal and professional conducts which may include dress codes, use of titles, and seating arrangements. German negotiators consider formality and use of surname as signs of respect.

In contrast, negotiators from informal cultures have little concern with negotiation etiquette. They adhere to a more loosely defined set of rules and are tolerant of those who deviate from norms, believing there are multiple ways to respond appropriately to a particular situation.

1.10 Styles of Communication 交流方式

Styles of communication refer to the degree to which negotiators rely on nonverbal cues to convey and to interpret intentions and information in business negotiation. High-context cultures depend more on the contextual cues in communication than low-context cultures.

Low-context cultures prefer explicit and direct communication. Negotiators from these cultures strive to use precise and frank words and intend them to be taken literally. North America and much of Western European countries prefer this type of communication. They are also direct and honest when they have negative evaluations about the other party. The Russians are also direct and factual in communication.

In contrast, high-context cultures put less emphasis on the literal meanings of the verbal messages and tend to use indirect, ambiguous and understated language. Words are not so important as context, which may include the speaker's gestures, postures and other environmental cues. They expect the other party to understand their unarticulated intentions and feelings through these cues. Negotiators from Asia, Africa, South America and much of the Middle East countries normally use this style of communication.

1.11 Nature of Persuasion 说服方式

Nature of persuasion refers to the type of evidence negotiators use to develop persuasive arguments. There are basically two types of evidence: facts and affection. On the one hand, in some cultures, negotiators tend to draw on empirical facts and linear logic to convince the other party. Evidence used to support persuasive arguments includes scientific results, professional standards, costs, market value, etc. German negotiators, for example, tend to stick to the facts in negotiations.

On the other hand, affective negotiators tend to use abstract theory, ideals, references to status and relationships and appeals to sympathy. This type of evidence includes equal treatment, moral standards, tradition and reciprocity.

1.12 Types of Satisfactory Agreement 满意的协议形式

Types of satisfactory agreement refer to the preferred forms of agreement between the parties. It can be formal written contracts or informal oral agreements.

In some cultures negotiators favor formal written contracts because contracts clearly specify rights and obligations, as well as the penalties that one party can extract if the other party fails to perform. Written contracts are believed to provide legal protection so that the parties may minimize the risk of business loss. German businessmen have the reputation of adhering to the contract, and regard it unacceptable that the other party does not comply with the contract.

In other cultures negotiators favor informal agreement because they stress the historical and social context of a relationship. They feel that the definite written contract terms are too rigid to allow a good relationship to develop. It is especially difficult for new relationships to expect and document every conceivable contingency. Negotiators tend to regard the contract as a rough guideline, not because they want to evade responsibility, but because relationship is much more important than the contract.

Key Terms

1. intercultural business negotiation 跨文化商务谈判

跨文化商务谈判指的是在不同文化间的商务活动中，当事人为了协调彼此的商务关系，满足各自的商务需要，通过协商洽谈以争取达成某项商务交易的行为和过程。不同国家和地区的政治经济体制和社会文化背景均有所不同，因而影响谈判的因素更为复杂多变，谈判难度也更大。

2. distributive negotiation 分配式谈判

分配式谈判也称为竞争型谈判或输赢谈判。在此类谈判中，双方的目标常有根本和直接的冲突。资源是固定且有限的，谈判者通常采用非赢即输的策略，全力以赴赢得竞争，打败对方，使自己的利益最大化。

3. integrative negotiation 整合式谈判

整合式谈判也称为合作型谈判或双赢谈判。在此类谈判中，双方的目标并不互相排斥。一方实现目标并不排斥另一方实现自己的目标，也不会损害另一方的利益。谈判者相互合作，努力寻求使双方都能取得进展并实现目标的解决方案，共同获得利益。

Glossary

construe	*v.* 解释；分析
predisposed	*adj.* 倾向于
capitalize	*v.* 估计……的价值；使资本化；利用；积累资本
trade-off	*n.* 妥协；权衡；交易

rapport	*n.*	融洽关系；友好关系
consensual	*adj.*	经双方同意的；一致同意的
assertive	*adj.*	观点明确的；坚决主张的
monochronic	*adj.*	单向计时的
polychronic	*adj.*	多向计时的
propensity	*n.*	倾向；偏爱
unarticulated	*adj.*	未表达的；不善于表达的；不相连接的
empirical	*adj.*	经验主义的；凭经验的；以观察或实验为依据的
reciprocity	*n.*	互惠；相互作用；相互性；互给
extract	*v.*	选取；获得
conceivable	*adj.*	可想到的；可能的
contingency	*n.*	可能性；偶发事件

Comprehension Questions

1. What is intercultural negotiation? What factors should be taken into consideration in intercultural negotiation?
2. What are the features of distributive and integrative negotiation?

2. Negotiation Strategies 谈判策略

Due to such elements as culture, background and education, negotiators tend to have their own characteristic approaches in negotiation. We have identified five basic strategies for conducting intercultural business negotiations: avoiding, accommodating, controlling, collaborating and compromising.

2.1 Avoiding 回避

The negotiators adopting this strategy show little interest in whether they attain their own outcomes, as well as little concern about whether the other party obtains his or her outcomes. They tend to ignore the entire dispute, or some specific issues, at least for some time, expecting the dispute may disappear naturally in the future. They use tactics to sidestep or postpone an issue or withdraw altogether from what they regard as a threatening situation. Sometimes this strategy results in a high degree of frustration for both sides in the negotiation. Therefore, it is generally regarded as a negative strategy.

Generally speaking, collectivist cultures tend to take avoiding strategy when conflicts arise, while individualistic cultures tend to be confrontational.

2.2 Accommodating 迎合

The negotiators show little interest or concern in whether they attain their own outcomes, but they are quite interested in whether the other party attains their outcomes. Accommodating involves lowering one's own aspirations to "let the other win" and gain what they want, at least for the present. Negotiators choose this strategy when they want to get the matter over with quickly and less expensively. They also tend to adopt their counterpart's approach of negotiations if they are familiar with the other culture and feel comfortable with their approach.

Generally speaking, individualistic cultures do not use this strategy often since they have high expectations about personal achievements. Comparatively, collectivist cultures tend to use accommodating strategy more often since they stress long-term relationship. They believe temporary accommodation is sometimes necessary and beneficial to build relationships.

2.3 Controlling 支配

The negotiators taking this strategy normally pursue their own outcomes strongly and show little concern for whether the other party obtains his or her desired outcomes. The negotiators take necessary steps to ensure that their goals are met. They believe that if they can force negotiations to operate according to their cultural terms, the other party will be disadvantageous in discussions of substantive issues.

Controlling strategy is commonly used and even encouraged in individualistic cultures, since their negotiation goals are largely task-based and only for a short term. In contrast, collectivist cultures do not encourage confrontation with their counterparts in conflicts, which they believe will damage their relationship and inhibit their long-term cooperation.

Case 3

An American manager was sent to China by his company to negotiate a contract with a Chinese company. When they were at a meeting, the American manager said to the Chinese manager: "I don't like what you said." The Chinese manager interpreted it as a personal insult.

In China, people would be more polite, perhaps by telling the person in private, or by making a suggestion, rather than by confronting it in public.

(Adapted from: 庄恩平. 跨文化商务沟通教程：阅读与案例[M]. 上海：上海外语教育出版社，2014.)

2.4 Collaborating 整合

The negotiators taking this strategy show high concern for attaining their own outcomes and high concern for whether the other party attains his or her outcomes. Collaborative principle negotiations aim to reach a solution beneficial to both parties by way of stressing interests and value but not by way of haggling. Both parties actively pursue approaches to maximize their joint outcome from the conflict.

Collaborating is believed to be the most effective strategy in negotiations. All cultures attach great importance in the use of this strategy in order to attain their goals in negotiations.

2.5 Compromising 妥协

This strategy represents a moderate effort to pursue one's own outcomes and a moderate effort to help the other party achieve his or her outcomes. The negotiators adopting this strategy look for an expedient, partially satisfactory middle ground. They are willing to make concessions in order to make a deal.

Different cultures take different attitudes towards compromise. In some countries such as the United States, the United Kingdom and China, compromise is understood as natural in negotiations. However, in such countries as Iran and Russia, compromise has a negative cultural connotation. It is against their principle of doing things. Therefore, they tend to refuse making compromise in negotiations.

Key Terms

1. strategy consideration 策略选择

策略的选择对于谈判至关重要，对谈判的结果具有决定性的作用。在谈判中可以选择单种策略，也可以依据谈判进程的发展结合运用多种策略。影响策略发挥作用的主要因素有谈判次数、双方实力的对比、本次交易的重要性、时间因素及谈判资源等。

2. principle 原则

谈判要有原则，需要原则进行指导。谈判的最佳结果是双赢（win-win），双赢的实现需要坚持系统观念。党的二十大报告指出，万事万物是相互联系、相互依存的。只有用普遍联系的、全面系统的、发展变化的观点观察事物，才能把握事物发展规律。我们要善于通过历史看现实、透过现象看本质，把握好全局和局部、当前和长远、宏观和微观、主要矛盾和次要矛盾、特殊和一般的关系，不断提高战略思维、历史思维、辩证思维、系统思维、创新思维、法治思维、底线思维能力，只有如此才能在谈判中实现互利共赢。

Glossary

sidestep	*v.* 回避；躲避；绕开
confrontational	*adj.* 对抗的；挑衅的
inhibit	*v.* 抑制；禁止
expedient	*adj.* 应急有效的；权宜之计的

Comprehension Questions

1. What are the common strategies in intercultural business negotiations?
2. What are the cultural differences in strategy selection?

3. Phases of Negotiation 谈判的过程

Generally speaking, the negotiation process can be divided into 5 phases: preparation, relationship building, opening, bargaining and closing.

3.1 Phase One: Preparation 第一阶段：准备

Careful preparations are of vital importance in negotiations across cultures. The preparatory work includes gathering background information, selecting team members and negotiation planning.

3.1.1 Gathering background information

Background research is the most fundamental part for the negotiation preparation. Background information includes both general information about the other culture and specific information about the other party.

General information includes the legal and judicial systems, the financial system, the size of the market and local standards, the availability of skilled labors, facilities, equipments and materials, etc. Relevant specific information about the other party includes their etiquette, customs, history, negotiation styles, their resources, issues, interests and needs, their targets and so on.

3.1.2 Selecting team members

Negotiation is a team sport. Generally speaking, a negotiation team consists of a team leader, professionals and an interpreter. The team is responsible for unifying the strategy, tactics and overall style to be used in the negotiation. Professionals should be experts in commercial, technical, financial and legal areas. Interpreters should be able to judge correctly the intention of the speaker and convey the meaning and intention appropriately and faithfully.

3.1.3 Negotiation planning

The planning of negotiations mainly consists of 3 steps. First, the negotiators should define the issues, giving an analysis to the issues to be discussed in the negotiation and deciding the sequence of them. Priorities should be given to more important issues. Then the resistance point should be set. For the seller, the resistance point is the lowest price they could accept for the goods; for the buyer, the resistance point is the highest price they will pay. Finally, the target point and the asking price should also be defined. The target point refers to the price one realistically expects to achieve in negotiation and the asking price refers to the best deal one can hope to achieve.

3.2 Phase Two: Relationship Building 第二阶段：建立关系

In this phase the negotiating parties should get to know each other. A harmonious relationship between the parties is expected to be established. Both parties normally allow some time in their schedules for such relationship building. This process usually takes the form of social events, tours, ceremonies, along with polite and informal conversations before meetings.

To establish an effective relationship, the negotiators should observe and respect different cultures. The time spent on relationship building varies from culture to culture. Negotiators from low-context cultures, such as the United States and Germany, often give little attention to this phase. They are more objective about the tasks at hand and usually want to get down to business immediately. In contrast, negotiators from high-context cultures, such as Asian and

South American countries, generally value interpersonal relationship in business. They spend much time on this phase of negotiation.

Case 4

William Smith, an American firm's manager in charge of marketing, scheduled a two-day trip to Rome to meet his Italian counterpart Alberto Moni and to have a discussion about the launch of a new product. Upon arriving in Rome, he first met with an expatriate Director, Ned Turner. Ned suggested that, apart from figuring out some details regarding the launch, he spend time getting to know Alberto and other members of the team personally and enjoying his visit in Italy.

Taking Ned's advice, William changed his plans for it became clear that two days would not be sufficient to accommodate all the discussions, long meals and entertainment that Alberto had planned to show Italian hospitality. On the fourth day, however, even though he had not gotten as far on the project as he had hoped, he was ready to leave on the first available plane.

William nearly lost his patience when Ned suggested that he delay his departure for one more day in order to meet some other members of the launch team in Italy who had just flown in from a conference. Instead, though, William held his tongue and gritted teeth at the prospect of sitting through another three-hour lunch.

(Adapted from: 庄恩平. 跨文化商务沟通教程：阅读与案例[M]. 上海：上海外语教育出版社，2014.)

3.3 Phase Three: Opening 第三阶段：开局

At the opening stage, negotiators greet each other, introduce their own positions and try to explore and understand their counterpart's intention or position in order to influence and manipulate the process of negotiation and obtain an advantageous position.

The objective at the opening stage may be described as exploration without commitment. Negotiators want to make sure that all the issues to be covered are stated, but at the same time they try to avoid any agreement or concessions.

Different approaches have been suggested in opening a negotiation. Some negotiators tend to build up a kind of resonance so that both parties can work together to push the negotiation forward under this friendly and harmonious environment. Others tend to convey their opinions frankly to make a breakthrough in the negotiation. Still others are more reserved at the beginning of the negotiation so that the other party will have a feeling of mystery and wonder what their intentions are.

At the end of the opening stage, the negotiators should know which parts of the offer their counterparts are likely or unlikely to accept so that they can predict the general form of the optimum bargain on each issue.

3.4 Phase Four: Bargaining 第四阶段：议价

This stage is considered the most important one in a negotiation. Each group tries to attain its goals through bargaining. The success of this step often depends on how well the parties understand each other's position, the ability of each to identify areas of similarity and difference, the ability to create new options, the willingness to work toward a solution that allows all parties to walk away feeling they have achieved their objectives and the ability to recognize and use certain tactics, such as promises, threats and so on (Luthans and Doh, 2014). A good agreement will optimize the interests of both parties, but it is more likely that one party will maximize its interests rather than the other's.

At this stage, the negotiating parties measure their own strength and strategies against each other. Each party should identify the extent of the importance of each issue so that trade-offs can be made and compromise can be reached.

Price is the most important issue in the process of bargaining. Next are payment terms and delivery. If the negotiation involves investment or technology transfer, then marketing, delivery of technical documentation, technical service and personnel training are also to be taken into consideration.

3.5 Phase Five: Closing 第五阶段：成交

The final stage of business negotiations involves reaching a final agreement. Negotiators from some cultures, such as the United States, would like to carry out this stage piecemeal, and make concessions and agreements on issues one at a time. Each issue, after it is resolved, is removed from the bargaining table, and interest is focused on the next. Asians and Russians, however, tend to negotiate a final agreement on everything, and few concessions are given until the end.

Once the negotiators reach an agreement, they normally would sign a contract. Both parties should make sure to have identical understanding of the terms in the contract. While signing a contract, negotiators should focus on the following clauses: commodity, quality, quantity, packing, unit price, shipment, insurance, terms of payment, claim, arbitration, etc.

Normally both parties expect to reach an agreement after the negotiation, but sometimes the negotiation ends in a draw, that is, there is no agreement reached. Declining a deal does not necessarily mean the negotiation is a failure. It may initiate the call for future talks once the deal-breaking aspects have been resolved. Although not ideal, it is respectable if it's done in a proper manner. Even if the negotiators have no intentions of ever dealing with each other in the future, maintaining the reputation within the international business community for levelheaded dealings is important.

Glossary

resonance	*n.* 共振；共鸣；反响
optimum	*n.* 最佳效果；最适宜条件；最适度
piecemeal	*adj.* 零碎的；逐个完成的；一件一件的
levelheaded	*adj.* 头脑冷静的；清醒的；稳健的

Comprehension Questions

1. How do negotiators deal with cultural differences in relationship building?
2. How can negotiators bargain successfully?

Extended Activities

Case Analysis

Case 1

Tom Forrest was an up-and-coming executive of an American company. He was sent to Japan to work out the details of a joint venture with a Japanese firm. During the first two weeks Tom felt that the negotiations were proceeding better than he had expected. He found that he had very good working relationships with the team of Japanese executives, and in fact, they had agreed on the major policies and strategies governing the new joint venture. During the third week of negotiations Tom was present at a meeting held to review their progress, which was chaired by the president of the Japanese firm, Mr. Hayakawa, who had recently taken over the presidency from his grandfather. The new president, who had been involved in most of the negotiations during the preceding weeks, seemed to Tom to be one of the strongest advocates of the plan that had been developed to date. The recently retired president, Hayakawa's grandfather, was also attending the meeting. After the plan had been discussed in some detail, the octogenarian past president proceeded to give a long soliloquy about how some of the features of this plan violated the traditional practices on which the company had been founded. Much to Tom's shock, Mr. Hayakawa did nothing to explain or defend the policies and strategies that they had taken weeks to develop. Feeling extremely frustrated, Tom then gave a fairly strongly argued defense of the plan. To Tom's further shock, no one else in the meeting spoke up in defense of the plan. The tension in the air was quite heavy and the meeting adjourned shortly thereafter. Within days the Japanese firm completely terminated the negotiations on the joint venture.

(Adapted from: 庄恩平. 跨文化商务沟通教程：阅读与案例[M]. 上海：外语教育出版社，2014.)

Questions for Discussion

1. What are the main differences between the U.S. and Japanese negotiators in this example?
2. Why did the negotiation fail?

Case 2

A U.S. corporation has sent a group of four people to meet with a group from a Russian organization. As the groups have had previous negotiations, the U.S. group is hoping to go home with an agreement. The first meeting lasts 12 hours and ends in a deadlock. After agreeing to meet the next day, one of the US negotiators notices the Russians leaving for an evening on the town. The next morning, the meeting is a repeat of the first, except that it is cut short so that the Russian negotiators can play golf. All agree to meet the next morning. The U.S. lead negotiator asks his company for time to wait out the Russians. Three weeks later (after many repeat meetings with no concessions), the Russians begin to make concessions.

(Source: Chaney L H, Martin S. Intercultural Business Communication[M]. NJ: Prentice Hall, 2004.)

Questions for Discussion

1. What do you know about the Russian culture that may explain the Russians' behavior?
2. Did the U.S. negotiators make the right move? Would pressure have made the Russians move faster?

Activities

Task 1

Suppose you are the sales manager of a shoe company who is going to negotiate with an American customer on the terms of price. Your latest product is the so-called "self-heating" boots. The boots themselves control the temperature inside automatically through friction and rubbing of your feet against the inner side of the boots, and your feet will never feel cold. Your sale price is FOB Shanghai, $65 a pair, but the price the American customer counter-offers is $55 a pair. Please act out the process of negotiation with your classmates.

Task 2

Suppose you are a manager of Shanghai Leather Shoes Factory, and Clarks Leather Shoes Factory from Britain intends to run a joint venture with you. Clarks will send a group of 5 people to Shanghai for field investigation and for a possible negotiation. How are you going to prepare for the possible negotiation? Act out the process of negotiation with your classmates.

Further Reading

How to Resolve Cultural Conflict: Overcoming Cultural Barriers at the Negotiation Table

Research shows that deal-making across cultures tends to lead to worse outcomes as compared with negotiations conducted within the same culture. The reason is primarily that cultures are characterized by different behaviors, communication styles, and norms. As a result, when negotiating across cultures, we bring different perspectives to the bargaining table, which in turn may result in potential misunderstandings. Misunderstandings can lead to a lower likelihood of exploring and discovering integrative, or value-creating, solutions. Let's talk about the main causes of cross cultural negotiation failure.

Cultural conflict in negotiations tends to occur for two main reasons. First, it's fairly common when confronting cultural differences, for people to rely on stereotypes. Stereotypes are often pejorative (for example Italians always run late), and they can lead to distorted expectations about your counterpart's behavior as well as potentially costly misinterpretations. You should never assume cultural stereotypes going into a negotiation.

Instead of relying on stereotypes, you should try to focus on prototypes—cultural averages on dimensions of behavior or values. There is a big difference between stereotypes and prototypes.

For example, it is commonly understood that Japanese negotiators tend to have more silent periods during their talks than, say, Brazilians. That said, there is still a great deal of variability within each culture—meaning that some Brazilians speak less than some Japanese do.

Thus, it would be a mistake to expect a Japanese negotiator you have never met to be reserved. But if it turns out that a negotiator is especially quiet, you might better understand her behavior and change your negotiating approach in light of the prototype. In addition, awareness of your own cultural prototypes can help you anticipate how your counterpart might interpret your bargaining behavior. It's not just about being aware of their culture, but also how yours might be viewed.

A second common reason for cross-cultural misunderstandings is that we tend to interpret others' behaviors, values, and beliefs through the lens of our own culture. To overcome this tendency, it is important to learn as much as you can about the other party's culture. This means not only researching the customs and behaviors of different cultures but also by understanding why people follow these customs and exhibit these behaviors in the first place.

Just as important, not only do countries have unique cultures, but teams and organizations do, too. Before partaking in any negotiation, you should take the time to study the context and the person on the other side of the bargaining table, including the various cultures to which he belongs—whether the culture of France, the culture of engineering, or his particular company's corporate culture. The more you know about the client, the better off you will do in any negotiation.

(Source:https://www.pon.harvard.edu/daily/conflict-resolution/a-cross-cultural-negotiation-example-how-to-overcome-cultural-barriers/, abridged)

Keys

Unit 1 Understanding Culture, Communication and Intercultural Communication

Page 7 Comprehension Questions

1. How do scholars elaborate on culture?

The scope of culture is very inclusive. There are hundreds of definitions about culture. Many scholars have defined and understood culture in various ways for many years, and among those the definition Hofstede proposes is widely used. He states, "Culture refers to the cumulative deposit of knowledge, experience, beliefs, values, attitudes, meanings, hierarchies, religion, notions of time, roles, spatial relations, concepts of the universe and material objects and possessions acquired by a group of people in the course of generations through individual and group striving."

2. What are the elements of each layer of culture?

Culture can be presented at different layers of depth. Trompenaars describes a multi-layered model of culture in which three main areas are identified. The outmost layer of culture is easily observed and includes explicit products of a culture. The core is implicit and encompasses basic assumptions about life and the world. The middle layer is made of norms and values, and determines what behaviours are interpreted as right or wrong, good or bad. It is identified by some scholar as four main layers of culture that is known as "onion diagram". They are culture symbols, culture heroes, culture rituals and culture values.

3. What are the major characteristics of culture?

There are four major characteristics of culture. First, culture is learned. Second, culture is transmitted across generations. Third, culture is based on symbols. Fourth, culture is dynamic.

Page 12 Comprehension Questions

1. How is culture interrelated with communication?

Communication is viewed as an element of culture. Communication practices will definitely change as cultures are different. One particular culture leads to a particular mode of communication.

2. How do scholars define communication? And how do you define it?

It is not easy for scholars to give communication a unique definition. The definition put forward by J. T. Wood is accepted by many people, "communication is a dynamic, systematic progress in which meanings are created and reflected in human interaction with symbols". You can express your own understanding of communication.

3. What are the basic types of communication?

There are four basic types of communication: verbal communication, nonverbal communication, written communication and visual communication.

4. Can you describe how communication occurs?

A basic communication process consists of seven major components: sender, message, encoding, medium, receiver, decoding and feedback. Sender first makes use of symbols and organizes them, which is the process of encoding, to convey the message to others by an appropriate medium. Next, receiver tries to convert the symbols received into meanings and extract the content of message, which is the process of decoding. Last, feedback is very necessary. It is any response to a communicated message.

Page 16 Comprehension Questions

1. Is intercultural communication identical to cross-cultural communication? Please explain the reasons.

The term "cross-culture" is always misunderstood as "intercultural communication"; however, the highlights of two terms are not the same. The term "cross-culture" is used in the intercultural literature to refer to the communication process that is comparative in nature, while the term "intercultural" is used to refer to the communication process between members of different cultural communities.

2. What are the main barriers in intercultural communication?

There are five main barriers in intercultural communication: language, negative stereotypes, prejudice and discrimination, ethnocentrism and values.

3. How are stereotype, prejudice and discrimination connected with each other?

It is thought that stereotype leads to prejudice, and prejudice leads to discrimination, and then discrimination leads to exclusion and inequality. They are interrelated and unidirectional, but all of them are deadly threats toward intercultural communication.

Page 17 Extended Activities

Case Analysis

Case 1

Questions for Discussion

1. Some Yulin people argue that it is their old tradition to eat dog meat. Are they wrong to keep their tradition?

Different cultures have different traditions that have been shaped for many years and passed down from generation to generation. We cannot easily draw a conclusion that they are right or wrong. Different traditions take their own forms under different circumstances. Eating dog meat is an old tradition of people in southern and northeast China. In the two regions of China, it was said that dog meat could provide good nutrition for people and ward off diseases, and thus they have been keeping this tradition up to now. However, we cannot say these people who eat dog meat are cruel or uncivilized just because they cling to this tradition.

2. There is a serious conflict between people who love dogs and Yulin people who love eating dog meat. What suggestions would you offer to mediate or resolve this conflict?

People in most Western countries love dogs and raise dogs like their family members. Therefore, they cannot bear that dogs are eaten and strongly oppose this tradition. Just as we have mentioned above, we cannot violently blame Yulin people for this tradition. It will take some time to get rid of a specific tradition. What we need to do is to enhance Yulin people's awareness of humane treatment of dogs. We can see that more and more people in Yulin are doing so and some of them have raised dogs as their pets. As for people who love dogs, they have the right to prevent dogs from being killed and eaten, but they should take moderate and effective measures, such as community advocacy and public-service advertisement.

Case 2

Questions for Discussion

1. What is the employment situation of women in Saudi Arabia? And what causes this consequence?

Women in Saudi Arabia are not well employed. They usually work in all-women factories or in lingerie and cosmetics shops. Unlike non-Muslim countries, Saudi Arabia strictly sticks to Muslim law that sets many restrictions on women. One of the restrictions is to forbid women to meet any men alone except those in their family. Otherwise, women will get severe punishment. Therefore, it is very inconvenient and impractical for women to work outside.

2. If you were a female foreigner in Saudi Arabia, would you behave the way you would do in your country? And why?

There is a saying "when in Rome, do as the Romans do". If a female foreigner plans to visit Saudi Arabia, she cannot behave as she does in her own country. She should learn basic customs or traditions of this country and get ready for everything in advance. When setting foot on Saudi Arabia, she should adjust her manners and clothes to make her look like a Saudi Arabian woman. Bear in mind that clothes showing too much skin are not appropriate; or else, it is very likely to kick up harassment. When meeting men, she should be more restrained and does not behave very openly.

Activities

1. Discussions (Omitted)
2. Group Work (Omitted)

Unit 2 Cultural Patterns and Communication

Page 28 Comprehension Questions

1. Use examples to explain the metaphor "culture values".

Values tend to be the basis of all the decisions we make and provide standards for us to evaluate our own and others' actions, and they are also a learned organization of rules for making choices and for resolving conflicts.

2. Can you use examples to explain culture values in international business?

Values are useful in explaining and understanding cultural similarities and differences in behaviors. Thus, it can enable managers to interact effectively with others whose values and behaviors are different.

Page 36 Comprehension Questions

1. Define Hofstede's five value dimensions.

power distance; individualism/collectivism; masculinity/femininity; uncertainty avoidance; long/short-term orientation

2. Please list several countries where men are expected to hold the primary jobs and women are expected to remain at home and raise families.

Japan, Austria, Mexico and Argentina

Page 39 Comprehension Questions

1. How do you define Kluckhohn and Strodtbeck's five value orientations?

Kluckhohn and Strodtbeck have the conclusion that people turn to their culture for answers to the following five questions: (1) What is the character of human nature? (2) What is the relation of humankind to nature? (3) What is the orientation toward time? (4) What is the value placed on activity? (5) What is the relationship of people to each other?

2. What is the value placed on activity?

Kluckhohn and Strodtbeck detailed the common modes of activity expression as being, being-in-becoming, and doing.

Page 44 Comprehension Questions

1. What are the characteristics of the high-context culture?

1. Long-term relationships.
2. People almost enjoy the same norms or values.
3. Strong boundaries—who is accepted as belonging vs. who is considered an "outsider".
4. Dense, intersecting networks and long-term relationships, strong boundaries, relationships more important than tasks.
5. Most of the information is in the physical world or in individuals.
6. Knowledge is situational and relational.
7. People value group identity orientation and covert communication codes and maintain a homogeneous normative structure with high cultural demand characteristics.
8. Decisions and activities focus around personal face-to-face relationships, and often around a central person who has authority.
9. A large portion of the message is left unspecified and needs to be accessed through the context.
10. People judge what someone is talking about not only by what he is saying but also by the context in which the message occurs.
11. More knowledge is below the waterline—implicit, patterns that are not fully conscious, hard to explain even if you are a member of that culture.

2. In what context "yes" can mean "yes" but probably mean "no"?

In high-context cultures, what people mean is judged not only by their words but also by the context in which the message occurs.

Page 44 Extended Activities

Case Analysis

Case 1

1. Why does the Canadian employee turn in his resignation?

Because the Canadian employee takes what means great concern to Chinese as distrust.

2. What kind of response may a Chinese employee have if a boss shows great concern for him or her?

They will be very happy because his/her boss has given great attention to his/her job.

3. What are the reasons of this communication barrier?

Because Chinese boss assumes unconsciously that the Canadian are more similar to Chinese employees than they actually are. And all these communication barriers are derived from culture differences, which appear not only in life but also in work.

Case 2

1. Why did the translator think no translation was necessary when an American engineer answered "one meter"?

Because the American engineer raised his hand with his index finger pointing upward.

2. Does the index finger represent the same number in America and Germany?

No.

3. Can you use this example to explain that encoding and decoding are the areas where miscommunication takes place?

Different gestures have different meanings in different areas.

Activities (Omitted)

Unit 3 Managing Intercultural Conflicts

Page 52 Comprehension Questions

1. Use examples to explain the metaphor "intercultural conflicts".

The clashes between the U.S. values of individualism, directness and time consciousness, and the Japanese interests in face-to-face discussion and consensus building.

2. Can you list several examples about "intercutural conflicts"?

(Omitted)

Page 59 Questions for Discussion

1. What are the symptoms of culture shock?

(1) Physical symptoms of culture shock.

(2) Psychological symptoms of culture shock.

2. How many stages are there during the period of culture shock? What are they?

There are five stages during the period of culture shock, including the honey moon stage, the hostility stage, the recovery stage, the adjustment stage and the biculturalism stage.

3. Try to give some details of transition adjustments.

In this stage, people realize that the new culture has good and bad things to offer and it can be one of double integration or triple integration depending on the number of cultures that people have to process.

Page 63 Comprehension Question

Please list several methods about alleviating culture shock.

Learn throughout your stay, get involved, master simple tasks, try to understand, and so on.

Page 63 Extended Activities

Case Analysis

Case 1

Is the British student crazy about coffee so that he drinks ten cups of coffee at his tutor's home?

No, he isn't. The reason why he did this is because the hostess may constantly pour coffee into his cup.

Case 2

How do you understand this case? Should Li Hua get angry?

It's an English tradition and Englishmen do this in order to make them feel at home, so Li Hua shouldn't get angry.

Case 3

1. Why did Mr. White get so angry with Mr. Zhang?

Because Mr. Zhang was not focusing on his work at that time.

2. Can you figure out some differences between Westerners and Chinese from this case?

Westerners put more emphasis on individual's progress which contributes to the team. However, Chinese care more about the environment and the whole team.

Case 4

Could the Westerners understand Chinese modesty?

The Westerners couldn't understand Chinese modesty. They consider it as an insult to them.

Unit 4 Verbal Communication

Page 82 Comprehension Questions

1. Use examples or experience to distinguish the differences between Chinese and Western styles of greetings, partings and styles of compliment.

(Omitted)

2. Compare address forms, greetings, partings and different compliments in different occasions.

Different occasions: between family members/at the party/in a seminar.

Page 86 Comprehension Questions

1. Use examples or experience to distinguish the differences between Chinese and Western e-mail writing habits.

Address forms, punctuation, writing style, etc.

2. Try to write a business e-mail and summarize some common conjunctions and usage of words when writing e-mails.

   (Omitted)

Page 86 Extended Activities

Case Analysis

Case 1

1. What happened to Vijay?

   The language Vijay learned at school is different from what is actually used in the daily life.

2. Why is this kind of phenomenon occurred around the oversea students?

   (Omitted)

Case 2

1. Distinguish the differences among the three scenes.

   (1) American and American: direct with purpose and purpose fulfilled

   (2) Chinese and Chinese: indirect with purpose and purpose fulfilled

   (3) American and Chinese: direct versus indirect and purpose unfulfilled

2. Explain the reasons.

   Aspects from culture differences, history and background (general or personal).

Unit 5 Nonverbal Communication

Page 95 Comprehension Questions

1. Which is more important, verbal communication or nonverbal communication? Explain why.

   Verbal and nonverbal communications are both very important to us. They coordinate with each other and help people express themselves much more clearly.

2. Role play: use nonverbal expressions only and perform a real-life situation.

   (Omitted)

Page 104 Comprehension Questions

1. How do we Chinese people use eye contact in communication?

For some Chinese people (shy, not confident, culture, custom, etc), it is unaccustomed to look into other people's eyes in communication.

2. Use examples or experience to distinguish the meanings of different gestures and postures in different countries.

(Omitted)

Page 106 Comprehension Question

Use different voice quality and vocalization to express a sentence.

(Omitted)

Page 109 Comprehension Questions

1. Find more object factors that affect interpersonal communication.

Attractiveness and the face, body shape, height, body image, body color, body hair (hair-style), etc.

2. Find some dressing taboos in different countries and explain the reasons.

Women use to veil their faces before going into public in Islamic countries.

Page 114 Comprehension Questions

1. Use examples or experience to explain the space you keep in your daily life.

(Omitted)

2. What do you think of the time concept of polychronic-time people?

(Omitted)

Page 114 Extended Activities

Case Analysis

Case

1. What triggered this student's utterance?

The inappropriate use of gesture of President Bill Clinton. In Chinese culture, pointing finger at others is considered as impolite.

2. What should we do when we encounter a different culture?

First, get yourself prepared by using Internet or reading some books in order to have a basic idea about other cultures. Second, if you accidentally offend other culture's taboo, apologize and ask the local people what to do in such circumstance. Third, try to be open to other cultures and bear in mind that every culture is valuable in some way.

Unit 6 Business Customs and Etiquette

Page 120 Comprehension Questions

1. What are business customs and etiquette?

Etiquette is ethical and socially acceptable behavior regarding professional practice or action among the members of a profession in their dealings with each other. Business etiquette and custom are expected behaviors and expectations for individual actions within a society, group, or class and within a place of business. It involves treating coworkers and employers with respect and courtesy in a way that creates a pleasant work environment for everyone.

2. How do handshakes vary accordingly in different countries and cultures?

Handshake is customary in many countries of the world. Many countries like China, India, Egypt, Finland, Britain, Germany, US, Nigeria, Kenya, etc., all consider handshake as a norm in interpersonal communications. Please check the following table "Handshakes by Culture" for detailed examples:

Handshakes by Culture

Culture	Type of Handshake
American	Firm
Asian	Gentle (shaking hands is unfamiliar and uncomfortable for some; the exception is the Korean, who usually has a firm handshake)
British	Soft
French	Light and quick (not offered to superiors); repeated on arrival and departure
German	Brusque and firm; repeated on arrival and departure
Latin American	Moderate grasp; repeated frequently
Middle Eastern	Gentle; repeated frequently

Page 122　Comprehension Question

What are superstitions and taboos in business world?

Superstitions are beliefs that are inconsistent with the known laws of science or what a society considers to be true and rational. Taboos are practices or verbal expressions considered by a society or culture as improper or unacceptable.

Page 124　Comprehension Questions

1. How do business persons spend holidays or holy days in overseas countries?

To businesspeople who conduct business with overseas countries, it is highly recommended to learn about other cultures' holidays and holy days, because during these days celebration is on and business may not be conducted at all.

2. What are the differences to celebrate holidays or holy days across different cultures?

For example, the New Year is celebrated in almost every part of the world. However, the nature, duration and time of celebration may vary greatly from country to country. For example, the date of Chinese Lunar New Year (Spring Festival) varies every year; while in Mexico, the two-week period including Christmas and New Year's Day is not a good time to conduct business nor is the two-week period prior to Easter, as business people are usually traveling with their families during this time.

Page 125　Comprehension Questions

1. What is bribery?

Bribery is the act of offering someone money or something valuable in order to persuade them to do something for you.

2. What measures do you know the countries take to deal with bribery?

For example, some countries have established laws to fight against bribery, for example, America has the most restrictive laws against bribery. In America, companies found guilty of paying bribes to foreign officials can be fined up to $1 million, and guilty employees may be fined up to $10,000 (Engholm, 1991).

Page 126　Comprehension Questions

1. Is there something common in exchanging business card among different cultures? If the answer is yes, then what is it?

When meeting with foreign business people, it is better to prepare a bilingual card and present it with the target language translation side up.

2. What are the differences in exchanging business card among different cultures?

In different cultures and countries, people present their business cards differently. In the United States, it might be normal for people to glance at the card they get and put it away promptly in the pocket. Whereas in Japan, this behavior can be considered very rude, for Japanese people consider it polite to examine the card carefully and make some comments before they put it away. Besides, Japanese as well as Koreans present their cards with both their hands, so it is better for foreigners to do in the same way. In Northern Europe, people are respectful of age, so include your company's date of establishment on your business card when the company's history is a long one (Turkington, 1999). Australian businesspersons do not usually carry business cards; thus, when you offer them your cards, you may not receive one in return. In Latin American countries, business titles are important, so be sure to include them on your business cards (Moran, Harris, & Moran, 2011).

Page 128 Comprehension Question

What are the positions and status of business persons in different cultures?

Social statuses can also be defined as those that are fixed for an individual at birth. Ascribed statuses that exist in all societies include those based upon sex, race, ethnic group and family background. Social position is the position of an individual in a given society and culture. A given position (for example, the occupation of priest) may belong to many individuals. Social positions influence social status. Social positions an individual may hold fall into the categories of occupation (medical doctor, academic lecturer), profession (member of associations and organizations), family (parent, sibling, etc), hobby (member of various clubs and organizations), among others. An individual is likely to create a personal hierarchy of such positions, where one will be a central position while the rest are peripheral positions.

Acknowledgment of the attendees' social status and their corresponding positions may show them proper respect, avoid unnecessary misunderstanding and embarrassment, and contribute to the success of intercultural communication encounters. Definitions of social class vary greatly from country to country and culture to culture. People in different parts of the world have their own distinct way of identifying the classes.

Page 131 Comprehension Question

What is electronic communication etiquette?

Electronic communication may include the telephone calls and cyber communication. Good telephone manners and following rules of online communication may avoid unnecessary embarrassment and misunderstanding and help enhance credibility.

Page 134　Comprehension Questions

1. What are the features of dining practices in Asia, America and Europe?

In many parts of Asia, people usually use chopsticks rather than knives and forks. Chopsticks are placed on the chopstick rest at the conclusion of the meal (or when pausing during the meal); they should not be placed in an upright position in the rice bowl (Martin & Chaney, 2012; Sabath, 2002).

The main meal in America is in the evening instead of noon. What's more different from Europeans is that Americans prefer a business meeting during breakfast time. Another US business custom questioned by people in other cultures is the lengthy cocktail "hour" before dinner. European countries still follow a common eating style called the Continental eating style. Actually Europeans ate in the same way with Americans until around 1850, and then the European upper class began to use the forks and knives differently, with the fork always in the left and the knife in the right hand. They use the knife to push food onto the back of the fork, and then move the food into the mouth with the tines of the fork down.

2. How do the dining practices vary from culture to culture?

The differences in dining practice mostly result from different diet culture. Different dining etiquette, dietary concept and dietary content can impact the differences. It is necessary to fully understand the different culture. The differences in dining practice may reflect in tableware, arrangement and atmosphere of banquet.

For example, Chinese people use chopsticks which can bring about all families sitting round the table, while people from Western countries who use fork and knife will bring about shared-food system. The differences of tableware between Chinese and Western countries are related to the environment around us.

Page 135　Comprehension Question

What situations require tipping?

Common situations that require tipping may include travelling, dining in fancy restaurants, and summoning cabs.

Page 136 Extended Activities

Case Analysis

Case 1

1. What are the main differences in business etiquette and customs between Chinese business persons and Iranian business persons?

In this case, firstly, Chinese businessmen have a strong sense of time with very tight schedules. In comparison, the Iranian business persons usually have a comparatively weak sense of time. Secondly, the dressing habits of the two countries are also different. Thirdly, the table manners are distinctive.

2. Why do the two parties have no longer substantive talks?

Because Chinese businessmen do not follow the Iranian customs and etiquette.

Case 2

1. Try to talk about the important role in business cards for today's business contacts combined with Ms. Wang's mistakes.

Business cards are cards bearing business information about a company or individual. They are used to be shared during formal introductions as a convenience and a memory aid.

2. Please think about how to show business cards correctly.

Firstly, gracefully taking your business card out of a professional looking case says that you are organized. Secondly, present and receive with both hands. When you present your business card with two hands, you are humbling yourself and asking the other person to accept your card. When you accept a business card with two hands, you are elevating the other person and showing gratitude for receiving their card. Thirdly, make sure the writing is facing the recipient. When presenting your business card, this will simply make it easier for the other person to read. Fourthly, when you receive the other person's card, study it and comment. Comment about their position in the company or simply repeat their name to show interest in them. If you are unsure how to pronounce their name, now is the perfect time to ask. Furthermore, don't immediately assume the first name that appears on the card is their family name: they have probably already switched their given and family names around for you.

Unit 7 Business Negotiation across Cultures

Page 151 Comprehension Questions

1. What is intercultural negotiation? What factors should be taken into consideration in intercultural negotiation?

Intercultural business negotiation is one that takes place between the interest groups from different countries or regions. Factors that should be put into consideration include culture, legal and political systems, the exchange value of international currencies, government regulations, social and political instability, ideology, external stakeholders, etc.

2. What are the features of distributive and integrative negotiation?

In a distributive negotiation, the negotiators try to maximize their own goals and interests, seeing one party's gains as the other's losses, while in an integrative negotiation, the negotiators aim to capitalize on the different interests of each party so as to find satisfactory trade-offs.

Page 154 Comprehension Questions

1. What are the common strategies in intercultural business negotiations?

Five basic strategies are identified for conducting intercultural business negotiations: avoiding, accommodating, controlling, compromising and collaborating.

2. What are the cultural differences in strategy selection?

Collectivist cultures tend to take avoiding strategy when conflicts arise, while individualistic cultures tend to be confrontational; collectivist cultures also tend to use accommodating strategy more often since they stress long-term relationship. Different cultures take different attitudes towards compromise. In some countries such as the United States, the United Kingdom and China, compromise is understood as natural in negotiations. However, in such countries as Iran and Russia, compromise has a negative cultural connotation.

Page 158 Comprehension Questions

1. How do negotiators deal with cultural differences in relationship building?

The negotiators should observe and respect different cultures. The time spent on relationship building varies from culture to culture. Negotiators from low-context cultures, such as the United States and Germany, often give little attention to this phase. In contrast, negotiators from high-context cultures, such as Asian and South American countries, generally spend much time on this phase of negotiation.

2. How can negotiators bargain successfully?

The success of this step often depends on how well the parties understand each other's position, the ability of each to identify areas of similarity and difference, the ability to create new options, the willingness to work toward a solution that allows all parties to walk away feeling they have achieved their objectives, and the ability to recognize and use certain tactics, such as promises, threats and so on.

Page 158 Extended Activities

Case Analysis

Case 1

1. What are the main differences between the U.S. and Japanese negotiators in this example?

In American culture, decisions are made by individuals, while in Japan, decisions are made collectively. Americans are direct in stating their opinions and tend to be confrontational, while the Japanese tend to avoid confrontations.

2. Why did the negotiation fail?

The negotiation failed mainly because Tom did not understand the Japanese negotiation style. At the beginning stage, Tom had a misconception that they had already made some agreements on the major policies and strategies. In the meeting, Tom argued with his counterparts, and expected some of them to give him support. He also ignored the authoritative power of the former president, whose opinion is still important in the negotiation.

Case 2

1. What do you know about the Russian culture that may explain the Russians' behavior?

Russians have different attitudes towards time from Americans. They tend to be more patient and stalled for time. Russians also tend to make concessions at the end of the negotiation.

2. Did the U.S. negotiators make the right move? Would pressure have made the Russians move faster?

Yes, the Americans made the right move. Pressure would not make the Russians move faster. They are believed to be determined and dogged negotiators.

Activities

Task 1

(Omitted)

Task 2

(Omitted)

References

布朗（H. Douglas Brown）（美）. 教学点津：跨文化交际教学实用方法[M]. 北京：清华大学出版社，2013.

常俊跃，吕春媚. 跨文化交际[M]. 北京：北京大学出版社，2011.

房玉清，姚颖. 跨文化交际实训（第二版）[M]. 北京：对外经济贸易大学出版社，2014.

董晓波. 跨文化商务交际[M]. 北京：北京交通大学出版社，2013.

杜学增. 中英文化习俗比较[M]. 北京：外语教学与研究出版社，2000.

高一虹. 语言文化差异的认识与超越[M]. 北京：外语教学与研究出版社，2000.

顾曰国. 跨文化交际[M]. 北京：外语教学与研究出版社，2000.

胡冰霞. 英语篇思维模式的差异及其对跨文化交际的影响[J]. 武汉交通科技大学学报，1999.

胡超. 跨文化交际实用教程[M]. 北京：外语教学与研究出版社，2016.

李君文. 东西文化价值观念对比与分析[J]. 湖南财经学院，2000.

卢晓静. 中西思维方式的差异对英汉语篇章的影响[J]. 福州师专学报，2002.

罗立彬. 商务谈判：双语版[M]. 北京：电子工业出版社，2013.

莫爱屏，莫凡. 跨文化交际教程[M]. 北京：北京大学出版社，2016.

秦勇，刘悦怡，齐环玉. 跨文化交际：经典阅读[M]. 广州：中山大学出版社，2014.

石定乐，彭春萍. 商务跨文化交际[M]. 武汉：武汉大学出版社，2008.

斯诺（Don Snow）（美）. 跨文化交际技巧：如何跟西方人打交道（学生用书）修订版[M]. 上海：上海外语教育出版社，2014.

瓦纳（Iris Varner）（美），比默（Linda Beamer）（美）. 全球化工作环境中的跨文化沟通（第三版）[M]. 上海：上海外语教育出版社，2006.

王维波，车丽娟. 跨文化商务交际[M]. 北京：外语教学与研究出版社，2014.

王玉环，李金珊. 跨文化交际学教程[M]. 北京：北京大学出版社，2011.

魏家海. 东西文化价值观的两重性与跨文化交际[J]. 西安外国语学院学报，2000.

熊丽君，刘学华. 跨文化交际学[M]. 上海：上海交通大学出版社，2010.

许力生，吴丽萍. 新编跨文化交际英语教程 教师用书[M]. 上海：上海外语教育出版社，2013.

许力生. 新编跨文化交际英语教程[M]. 上海：上海外语教育出版社，2015.

杨恒波. 跨文化交际教程[M]. 昆明：云南大学出版社，2014.

尹丕安. 跨文化交际：理论与实践[M]. 西安：西北工业大学出版社，2007.

余慕鸿，章汝雯. 商务英语谈判[M]. 北京：外语教学与研究出版社，2005.

张爱琳. 跨文化交际[M]. 重庆：重庆大学出版社，2011.

中共中央党史和文献研究院，中央学习贯彻习近平新时代中国特色社会主义思想主题教育领导小组办公室. 习近平新时代中国特色社会主义思想专题摘编[M]. 北京：党建读物出版社，中央文献出版社，2023.

中国共产党第二十次全国代表大会文件汇编[M]. 北京：人民出版社，2022.

庄恩平. 跨文化商务沟通教程：阅读与案例[M]. 上海：上海外语教育出版社，2014.

Bates, D. G., & Plog, F. (1990). *Cultural Anthropology* (3rd ed.). NY, USA: McGraw-Hill.

Beamer, L., & Varner, I. (2005). *Intercultural Communication in the Global Workplace*. New York: McGraw-Hill.

Chaney, L. H., & Martin., S. (2004). *Intercultural Business Communication*. Upper Saddle River, NJ: Prentice Hall.

Chryssochoou, X. (2004). *Cultural Diversity: Its Social Psychology*. MA, USA: Blackwell, Malden.

Cohen, R. (1991). Paraphrasing Tylor's Primitive Culture. *Negotiating across Cultures: Communication Obstacles in International Diplomacy*. Washington DC, USA: United States Institute of Peace.

Dance, F. E. X. & Larson, C. E. (1972). *Speech Communication: Concepts and Behavior*. NY, USA: Holt, Rinehart & Winston.

Filipowicz, G. (2004). *Zarządzaniekompetencjamizawodowymi*. PWE, Warszawa.

Gudykunst, W. B. (2004). *Bridging Differences: Effective Intergroup Communication* (4th, ed.). London, UK: Sage.

Hall, E. T. (1961). *The silent language*. New York: Premier Books.

Hall, E. T. (1966). *The Hidden Dimension*. NY, USA: Anchor Press/Doubleday.

Hall, E. T. (1977). *Beyond Culture*. Garden City, NY, USA: Anchor Doubleday.

Hoebel, E. A., & Frost, E. L. (1976). *Cultural Anthropology*. NY, USA: McGraw-Hill.

Hofstede, G. (1997). *Cultures and Organizations*. NY, USA: McGraw-Hill.

Hofstede, G. (2001). *Culture's consequences: Comparing values, behaviors, institutions and organizations across nations*. Beverly Hills, CA: Sage.

Hofstede, G. J. (2005). *Cultures and Organizations: Soft-ware of the Mind*. New York: McGraw-Hill.

Hofstede, G., Hofstede, G. J., & Minkov, M. (2010). *Cultures and Organisations, Software of the Mind, Intercultural Cooperation and its Importance for Survival-Software of the Mind*. NY, USA: McGraw-Hill Education.

Jacob S, McClintock MK, Zelano B, Ober C (*2002*) Paternally inherited HLA alleles are associated with women's choice of male odor. Nat Genet 30(2):175–179.

Jones, M. (2002). *Social Psychology of Prejudice*. Upper Saddle River, NJ, USA: Person Education.

Kędziora, M. (2013). *Rzeczowo o modziemęskiej*. Wydawnictwo SQN, Kraków.

Kerri, J. (2013). *Nonverbal communication and body language* (1st ed.). Cognella Academic Publishing.

Kluckhohn, C. K. (1949). *Mirror for Man: the relation of anthropology to modern life*. Berkeley, CA: Whittlesey House.

Kluckhohn, C. K. (1951). Values and value orientations in the theory of action. In T. Parsons and E. A. Shils (Eds.), *Toward a general theory of action*. Cambridge, MA: Harvard University Press.

Kluckhohn, F. R., & Strodtbeck, F. L. (1961). *Variations in value orientations*. Evanston, IL: Row, Peterson.

Kroeber & Kluckhohn (1952). Cited by Berry, J. W. In Fundamental psychological progress in intercultural relations (pp.181). In Landis, D., Bennett, J.M. & M. J. Bennett (Ed.) (2004), *Handbook of Intercultural Training*, 3rd ed. (pp.166-84). CA, USA: Thousand Oaks.

Luthans, F., & Jonathan D. (2014). *International Management: Culture, Strategy and Behavior*. McGraw-Hill Education.

Mandana S., & Marianne, G. (2014). *From gesture in conversation to visible action as utterance (essays in honor of Adam Kendon)*. Amsterdam/Philadelphia: John Benjamins Publishing Company.

Mark, L. K., Judith A. H., & Terrence, G. H. (2014). *Nonverbal communication in human interaction*. Wadsworth: Cengage Learning.

Martin, J. N., & Nakayama, T. K. (2005). *Experiencing Intercultural Communication*. New York: McGraw-Hill.

Mehrabian, A. (1995). *Nonverbal Communication*. Walter De Gruyter In.

Michael, A. (1984). *Bodily Language*. Methuen and Co. Ltd.

Michael A. G. (2015). *Public speaking basics* (revised edition). Lanham, Maryland: University Press of America.

Neil, T. (2015). *People skills* (4th ed.). Palgrave: Macmillan Education.

Pachter, B. (2013). *The Essentials of Business Etiquette: How to Greet, Eat, and Tweet Your Way to Success*. McGraw Hill Education, New York.

Pennington, D. C. (1986). *Essential Social Psychology*. London, UK: Edward Arnold.

Pietkiewicz E. (1998). *Protokółdyplomatyczny*. Wydawnictwo Prawnicze: Warsaw.

Porter, R. E., Samovar, L. A., & Stefani, L. A. (2000). *Communication Between Cultures*. Beijing: Foreign Language Teaching and Research Press.

Post, P., Post, A., Post, L., & Post, S. D. (2011, October). Emily Post's Etiquette (18th ed.). *Emily Post's Etiquette.* William Morrow.

Post, P., Post, A., Post, L., & Post, S. D. (2014). *The Etiquette Advantage in Business* (3rd, ed.). New York: Harper Collins.

Samovar. (1981). *Understanding Intercultural Communication*. Wadsworth.

Samovar, L. S., & Porter, R. E. (1982). *Intercultural Communication: A Reader* (6th ed.). CA, USA: Wadsworth, Belmont.

Samovar, L. A., Porter, R. E., & Stefani, L. A. (2000). *Communication Between Cultures*. Beijing, China: Foreign Language Teaching and Research Press & Brooks/Coles/Thomson Learning Asia.

Scherer, K. R., & Walbott, H. G. (1994). Evidence of Universality and Cultural Variation of Differential Emotion Response Patterning. *Journal of Personality and Social Psychology*, 66(2), 310-328.

Schneider, D. J. (2004). *The Psychology of Stereotyping*. London, UK: Guilford Press.

Spencer-Oatey, H. (2008b). Introduction. *Culturally Speaking: Culture, Communication and Politeness Theory* (2nd ed.). London, UK: Continuum.

Spencer-Oatey, H., & Franklin, P. (2010). *Intercultural Interaction: A Multidisciplinary Approach to Intercultural Communication*. Beijing, China: Foreign Language Teaching and Research Press & Palgrave MacMillan.

Ting-Toomey, S. (2007). *Communication Across Cultures*. Shanghai, China: Shanghai Foreign Language Education Press.

Trompenaars, F., & Turner, C. H. (1994). *Seven Cultures of Capitalism: Value Systems for Creating Wealth in Britain, the United States, Germany, France, Japan, Sweden and the Netherland*. London, UK: Piatkus.

Weiss, S. E., & Stripp, W. (1998). Negotiating with Foreign Businesspersons: An Introduction for Americans with Prepositions on Six Cultures. In S. Niemeier (Ed.), *The Cultural Context in Business Communication.* John Benjamins Publishing Company.

William, J. S. (1992). *Introduction to Speech Communication*. Harper Collins Publishers Inc.

Wood, J. T. (1989). *Gender Lives: Communication, Gender, and Culture*. CA, USA: Wadsworth Belmont.

http://communicationtheory.org/definitions-of-communication/.

http://www.buzzle.com/articles/four-types-of-communication.html.

http://www.managementstudyguide.com/components-of-communication-process.htm.

http://gbtimes.com/life/dog-meat-eating-festival-tradition-or-torture

http://schmidtgen.com/wordpress/2013/10/20/how-to-use-jr-sr-ii-iii-etc-with-cartoons